The Spirit Born People

Puran Singh

1926

PREFACE

These are the lecture notes for addresses I proposed to deliver to the Sikh youth of the Punjab. But as I am placed in the desert away from the towns where they gather, I let these go undelivered. And also because the Sikh youth are running in haste after shadows, turning their backs on the Sun of Suns, the *Guru*. This world of the Guru, the Beautiful, is different and their world how different; so to them the values of fiction and fact have been hopelessly interchanged. Still, I hope these addresses will reach them by and by.

And the Sikh youth is everywhere, the youth that has the disciple-consciousness, aspiring to love, the Beautiful, which alone is truly good, truly noble, and truly divine. The form Beautiful appearing once rarely in ages, and fascinating the disciple-consciousness and vanishing in the eternal background of the spiritual inner Infinite, is the Guru Beautiful, the Bridegroom; the disciple-consciousness thenceforward restless without that presence or the sense of that presence is *The Spirit Born People*,—or The Brides.

P.O. Chak 73/19
via Jaranwala (Punjab)

PURAN SINGH

CONTENTS

I.	The Discipleship	9
	1. Bhai Buddha	10
	2. Painde Khan	13
	3. Retie the Broken Ties	14
	4. The Spirit Born People	15
	5. Under a Hank of Hair	17
II.	The Spiritual Attitude	19
	1. Religion so-called	19
	2. The Farthest To-day	20
	3. Spiritual Attitude	24
	4. Nam Dev	25
	5. The King of the Purple Colour	27
	6. The Jealous God	30
	7. Kabir and His Wife Loi	31
	8. Lord Gauranga	33
	9. An unknown Sikh saint who cultivated his lands	34
	10. The Music of Universal Fellowship	34
	11. 'Bread', 'Woman' and 'Bridegroom'	36
	(a) *Bread*	37
	(b) *Woman*	43
	(c) *The Guru or the Divine Bridegroom*	47
III.	The Garden of Simrin	50
	1. 'The Name'	50
	2. Our Long Tresses	51
	3. The Agitated Doves	52
	4. Of equal dignity with the Stars	53
	5. The Guru-Personality Impersonal makes the Sangha	53
	6. Simrin is the Only Builder of Unselfish Personality	60
	7. The One Thing Needful	63
IV.	'Asa-Di-Var' of Guru Nanak	71
V.	The Message of 'Sukhmani' of Guru Arjun Dev	78
VI.	Readings from 'Sukhmani'— The Charmed Gem of Peace	85
VII.	The 'Japuji' of Guru Nanak	93
VIII.	Surta—Soul Consciousness	100
	1. The Divine Lamp	106
	2. The Spiritual Universe at the Back of the Man of Spirit who is Authorised	110
IX.	The Sword of Guru Gobind Singh	115
X.	Internationalism and The Sikhs	118

XI.	Notes on Art and Personality from The Sikh Viewpoint	129
XII.	'Guru Prasad'—By His Favour	143
XIII.	The Brothers of the Tress-Knot of Guru Gobind Singh	148
XIV.	The Doer of Good and the Toiler on Earth	156

I

THE DISCIPLESHIP

The title 'Sikh', 'The Disciple', was first given to us by Guru Nanak. We were mere corpses, he poured life into us. We were thus created anew by His love of us. He made us alive with our out-drawn love of Him and left us free. He freed us from the hatred of caste, colour and creed. He made us look straight at the sky towards the Infinite, he made us look upon the sun and the moon and the stars as our kith and kin. He did knit us with the Universe and he wove the design of the Infinite into the texture of our soul. He gave us then the universal music to sing; birds and animals to be our confidants, woods and rivers and hills to sing with us. This world that sat like a nightmare on us was thrown away: the new world was laid open before our eyes in His Vision. The veil was almost torn asunder and this spiritual universe of love was opened to our vision. And we were elevated from the valleys of darkness on to the sunlit heights. Peasants became poets by His touch. The enslaved womanhood was freed from its bondage of the soul. When the Ninth Guru, Guru Tegh Bahadur came to Amritsar, the priests shut the doors against the Master. He turned his back on the Golden Temple, the brick and mortar, and bore away the true Golden Temple in his heart as a holy vision. The Golden Temple would have gone for ever from Amritsar. But the Sikh ladies of Amritsar saw this danger. They, in their freedom, followed the Master and sang to Him His Hymns. He blessed them and blessed Amritsar. The Golden Temple was saved for this poor earth of ours by the freed Sikh womanhood.

This is the plain history. Our history is of the soul, all its events are of the soul. All truth for us is personal. We have not to prove it, we have to stand witness to it in our soul. By the title 'Sikh', he linked us with Himself forever. And we cannot tear ourselves away from Him. It would be misery for us if we turn our backs on Him.

1. BHAI BUDDHA

You remember how Bhai Buddha — The Brother Ancient — got the title. He saw his mother kindling a fire. And he saw that the smaller twigs caught fire first and the longer ones, a little later. And unlike us, the young men of to-day, who choose to live dull lives, mostly uninterested and unconcerned, that young man was much too sensitive. As the leaves of the sensitive plant are to the touch, so the little boy was sensitive to the touch of wonder. He wondered why the smaller twigs caught fire first. He was a genius. What is genius but that which responds with the sensitiveness of the sensitive plant to the Light of Heaven? He thought his mother would go to see Guru Nanak seated under the shade of a tree. Seeing Guru Nanak is like touching the fire of Heaven. Seeing Him is to be kindled like a star from a star. He thought his mother would follow, but it was he who must first catch that Gleam and burn with it.

With this inward realization of wonder, the young man did go to Guru Nanak.

At the sight of the Guru, he found he was wholly inflammable. His flesh and bones caught fire. The young man was called by the Guru. He heard his story and the Guru gave him the title of 'The Brother Ancient' — so young and yet so ancient in wisdom. Bhai Buddha is the 'Brother' — 'The Sikh'.

No historian or biographer can tell us what happened then to Bhai Buddha. Ordinary history gives corpses of events, it registers accurately the dead facts which are mostly wrong. History has no testimony for our soul. You may study a friend of yours for a long time and yet find all your conclusions about his character upset by stumbling over a kind act of his to you, and that one silent act of his may discover to you that he is your Messiah. History and biography are both lies, so far as these matters are concerned. Who can report the soul correctly, which, till to-day remains unrevealed and undescribed, for it is always a surprise and a revelation. Such matters are beyond our analysing intellects. But mark the effects. The whole life of Bhai Buddha thenceforward is a marvel. Living on a few grassy acres near Amritsar, with a few cows grazing by his side quietly, the 'Brother Ancient' lives self-enclosed, immersed wholly in the Guru. His lips pipe His Name. He fills himself with glory. The firmament revolves as a torch in his hand in the worship of the Beloved. His bosom throbs like that of a bird that trills a song. His hairs stand on end with ecstasy. His eyes are red, half-closed, rapt, vision-bound, wonder-bound, happy like the full-blown flower, and all so beautiful. And the continuousness of his kindled passion, shaking his day and night with joy, makes of him a radiant presence, a persuasive silence, a soothing influence, a peace incomparable shedding joy all around like the cloud, like the sun, like the moon, like the shade of a tree.

He lives in the wilderness, naming him. No heroic woman ever loved man more passionately than Bhai Buddha loved Guru Nanak. Constancy of love needs silent heroism. Intensity of pleasure comes to all animals during many a turn of life in this world. The sight of a woman may give that exquisite thrill; the finding of a treasure by a poor man might give him a foretaste of the paradise, the poet may feel inspired for a rare moment at the sight of the beautiful universe, but nothing comes near the grandeur of the sublime passion of Bhai Buddha who lives like a whole universe in himself. The exterior expression of this ecstatic life is stopped owing to the continuous imbibing of the Great Reality. The language has lost all unnecessary words; the sound has dropped the inanities of thought, the whole flesh has become the mind and having grown translucent has the opalescence of a mixed sheen of pearls and rubies. Bhai Buddha's humanity has turned into daily food for the Divine Flower that has burst in him. Bhai Buddha is burning like a lamp at the altar of Guru Nanak. Silent burning is the only artistic expression of such an infinite kind of disciple-personality — such was the reaction of Bhai Buddha towards Guru Nanak.

Perhaps, you might be led to think that, like the ancient Hindus, the 'Brother Ancient' had become a Saint, whose main concern was the contemplation of the pure, the Absolute, the *Brahman*. The type of blissful humanity, the Brother Ancient represents, is quite new. The bliss of Guru Nanak's Sikh waves in him like a vast ocean. But it is ever in motion, and yet wholly at rest in itself. The ineffable bliss of remembrance of Him has an infinite pang which it nestles within itself. This pang of love is manifested in the life of the disciple in different ways. It might take the shape of absolute forgiveness of a sinner, for in this acute pang, man is much too sweet for any revenge which, in many forms, is known on this earth as justice. The vision of justice in the self-consciousness of the disciple is forgiveness; there can be no other justice between man and man in the domain of discipleship, where love reigns and never hatred.

It might take the form of total self-sacrifice in peace or in war, or it might be content to live as beautiful as the lotus, doing without knowing, the greatest service to life that Pure Beauty can render.

It might take the form of a political revolution against tyranny, as it once did in the time of Guru Har Gobind and Guru Gobind Singh.

This bliss of the disciple is restless, with the human pain which moved Lord Buddha to compassion.

The Brother Ancient realizes his knowledge of sorrow when Guru Har Gobind went to Gwalior and was for a long time absent from Amritsar. Amritsar was always holy to him because of His Presence, but it became holier to him in an unspeakable anguish of separation from Him. In His absence, the Sikh worshippers came and went, but the Brother Ancient not seeing the Guru was restless, as fish out of water. The Brother Ancient lights a torch as the night falls and goes round the temple singing his pang of separation, in acute remembrance of Him, as if He had come to listen to the disciple in the Golden Temple. And He did come. Did He not tell Bhai Buddha on his return how he heard his love-cries, every evening while at Gwalior?

The Guru returns and transmutes the Torches of Separation, of the burning pain, into the Torches of Union, of the burning joy. The colour of the Temple changes. The Brother Ancient returns to his cloister and is mute again, happy like a child with his cows grazing on the turf.

2. Painde Khan

We see the very pang seeking to cool itself in a stream of burning lead, the disciples baring their breasts to bullets, to swords, and to bayonets. No snow can cool it down, nor can rivers wash it away. Death in His Name offers the cup of sweet companionship with Him through an intense ecstasy. Painde Khan, the beloved Sikh of Guru Har Gobind, turns a rebel, a traitor. He comes to fight with the Master. The Master allows the disciple the chance of giving him the first blow. But Painde Khan fails. He cannot give Him the cut of the combat. The Master's sword then wounds the disciple deep. Painde Khan falls from his horse. The sun is burning overhead, the sands are hot below. The Master lifts up his disciple, puts his head in His lap and shades the forgetful Painde Khan by His large shield. And the Master asks him, "Painde Khan, Thou art dying. Say thy *Kalma* now".

Painde Khan, the disciple, wakes up and says with his trembling lips, "My *Kalma* is Thy sword-cut, O Beloved! Thy word, my salvation. How intensely blissful is such death at Thy hands, O Lord of Love!"

This deep personal love that coppices again and again even when cut, is the symptom of discipleship and it comes to one when he is called by the Guru, 'The Sikh'.

3. Retie the Broken Ties

Man is weak. He is, when sincere, but a pilgrim to the Golden Temple. And the path of the pilgrim is full of difficulties. Sometimes hunger, thirst and nakedness and at others impertinent desires dim his faith and bend it beyond the limits of elasticity. Faith breaks, the vision is lost, the nectar of naming Him is spilled. Heavy darkness settles on his eyes, his limbs grow weary, his heart faints. And the disciple is as dead.

The Sikhs with Guru Gobind Singh in the fort of Anandpur would not obey him, for the siege of the enemy was long and unbreakable and the Master desired to hold on till the last. In His desire was victory. But the disciples would not obey Him. They deserted Him. Had they obeyed Him, all would have been different. But the great devotion for the Master was flaming in the peasant mud-huts of the Punjab. More than man, the Sikh women were in the same passionate love with Him, as the Mary and Martha of Palestine with the Messiah, in the olden times. Doors were closed against the deserters. There was no love for them after they left Him at Anandpur. All loving hearts were shut against them. But this act of the noble Sikh women kindled the extinguished hearts of the confused and weak disciples. The forty martyrs of our history shall ever stand peerless in the glory of self-sacrifice for Him. You remember when the sun went down, He went amongst the wounded and blessed them. One of the dying disciples asked not for life, asked not for kingdoms, but only begged that all his brothers who deserted Him and gave it in writing to Him, might be soul-knitted with the Guru, with the Glory of the Infinite and that the document might be torn. Guru Gobind Singh tears the document and forgives all—'Retie the broken ties' is one of our most stirring national songs.

4. THE SPIRIT BORN PEOPLE

The caravans of the Sikhs coming from different climes, and different directions and belonging to different castes are on their way to the 'Pond of Immortality' where they shall bathe in the sunshine of the Guru. Their eyes are tearing the distances of time to have a glimpse of Him. Guru Arjan Dev goes dad in a single black blanket, after the fashion of the Punjab peasantry with a repast for the disciples of Guru Nanak. Our mother Ganga, his noble consort, follows him with a basket of bread on her head. And they both distribute the way-side refreshments to the disciples and with it the Name. The Sikhs go singing to Amritsar and there is seated Guru Arjan Dev. They recognise Him as the devoted peasant who fed them on their way to Amritsar. This sweet spirit of comradeship, in this country of castes, differences, duality and morbid and sick imitations of the 'Great Renunciation', so infused by the Guru is unique. The Man is made *Sadh Sangat*. All saw the Image of the Guru in all hearts. Men disappeared but the Image of the Guru with the angelic beaming faces entranced the eyes of the disciples. And such a Guru lost individual meeting himself in his brothers and sisters, was the Guru's assembly of gods come on earth. The Guru and the Sikh intermingled and the sweet merging of the individual into the very universe of nature and man — the All becoming the image of One, and the One becoming the image of All — is the spirit of the Guru's *Sadh Sangat*. This assembly in His inspiration was unique. *Sadh* is the one lost, the *Sangat* is the one gained, as Many as the All. *Sadh Sangat*, thus, is the mystic body of the Guru. And the State and the Society became one in Him as the individual made infinite. And the Guru dwells in the spirit of this spirit-born Humanity. He has promised His meeting us in the meeting of this rare assembly of gods.

Assuredly we are yet far away from the Golden Temple that sings of the Beautiful.

How disgraceful for us that we call a mere assemblage of un-inspired men a *Sadh Sangat!*

Let me tell you, one disciple, he or she, if there be, is capable of burning a whole people with love and making them evergreen. And we *Sadh Sangat*, and yet so inert! Extinguished lamps emit no light. We are wholly wrong in distributing titles to ourselves. We no more go with any original thirst to the Founts of Inspiration. On the contrary, we are nourishing a stupid complacency and deadening our soul thereby and calling a life-long stupor, and indifference to the highest verities of our traditions of inspiration by many ornamental names. So did our Hindu fore-fathers and they sealed up all the fountains of life. We, too, if we rise not to our full moral stature, shall soon become fossils, not Sikhs.

Beware of the magic of Brahmanical philosophic analysis of everything, even the most secret and complex infinites of faith, life and love. It killed them, it shall kill you. Analysis is the opposite pole of feeling. I worship my mother, I love my wife, but what would they be if I wished to know them by analysis!

The pang of separation from the Guru becomes a lifelong pure sadness, noble, beautiful sorrow of human life in the very breath of the disciples.

> O Love! I can no more praise Thee.
> Thou hast wounded me too deep for song.
> I'd rather be sad of Thee, in tears,
> For thou art more beautiful than joy.

Wasting away in holy memory of Him is better religion than going to the temples and becoming redundantly glad by a meaningless ceremony. True worship is in the continuous pang for that Glory. Mere flower offering is a formality that kills the serious purpose fullness of love in empty theatricalities. All theatre and theatre-going, therefore, I say, leads us away from the genuine forms of true feeling. Feeling is always new, like the effects of the sky; its one moment is quite different from the next. Renunciation in that particular form as of Lord Buddha, is reality only there: in any other man's case it ceases to be 'feeling', it is only 'following'. Feeling alone is love, is art, is religion, 'following' is of no particular interest to the artistic seekers of That Noble Reality of a personal feeling.

The soul-pure figure of this pang spiritual which makes beauty a new glory everyday, is Rani Rajkor, the art-creation of a true disciple-character by Bhai Vir Singh, the great Sikh poet, in his *The Prince Beautiful,* written in Punjabi. She is the Sikh heroine. Her love is deep and silent and vital and painfully flourishes in the shade. In the glare it dies; much too Heavenly, much too musical to be announced so profanely. This relation of pangful love is between the Guru and the Sikh. All love has its sacred privacy and this too. In this love, art ceases and the artist grows to be the whole art.

5. Under a Hank of Hair

The Guru has buried the disciples under heaps of grass. He has concealed His handicraft in a hank of hair. Very irrational, they say. Possibly very superstitious. But superstitions preserve the life sparks more effectively than the reason of man. In the fleecy clouds is lightning. In our superstition of hanks of hair there is truth of His burning bosom divine. Christ in his Bride-braids is certainly more beautiful even as a man, as a woman-born, than a clean-shaven modern American face which is more in the image of the Dollar than of the sweet Jesus who is the comfort of so many distressed souls. The pendulum would swing. Fashions would give way to Love again. God would replace the Dollar, or elsewhere shall be the Man's Art, which is more of that lyrical leisure divine, of soul, of love. This haste, this machine-like man is far removed from His self, the Great Guru love. Our Truth, unlike that of the old Brahman, is not any mathematical balance of an endless denying of things. Our Truth is not a problem solved. Our Truth is but a lotus and the bee buzzing about, the cloud and the rain-bird crying for that pearl-like drop of life, the swan and the lake, the child and the mother, the cow and the calf. Our hymns centre round these metaphors and all human suffering is vindicated in a moment of this transitory Union, even if it be after ages. Meeting Him dispels all sorrow, but it is all sorrow without Him. His absence is as holy as His presence.

And countless such living statues of Holy *Simrin,* of Love's inspiration filling the whole Temple of this earth and its domes and galleries and diffusing the atmosphere of the individual peace into the crowned universe of such statues, is the Ideal of the Divine Society of men made angels by the Grace of His Love.

Assuredly in this kingdom of dream and vision, there is no place for duality, hatred and harm, so deeply ingrained in the animal man.

O Sikh young men! rise and fill yourselves' with this Glory. It makes you noble, bold and free, self-drunk, selfless, flower-like, sun-like. It sweetens you and your sweetness sweetens all life around you. At your sight, the lamb and the tiger must drink at the same pool. Perpetual spring must roll in you. You shall be the moral influence radiating peace, good-will, friendship, fellowship, life, vigour, vitality, in short, spirituality. You shall live in perpetual blossom, reconciled to the sorrow of life in a thousand new ways every day. Be ye a revelation to the world of man, of the gods that live in your hearts. Seekers after God retire to the woods. Show them they need not go to the woods, for the Guru made you the woods. Seeing you, you yourself, the very peace of woods, the freshness of the little rivulets chiming through them should come to all. Your long tresses shall provide the shade of the woods and their mystery.

II

THE SPIRITUAL ATTITUDE

1. Religion so-called

In olden days, religion was all the knowledge man had of himself and of the Universe. Knowledge of objects was also huddled up in the 'sacred literatures'. Astronomy and logic too came in religion. Social Hygiene and the individual's cleaning his own vestures was a part of religion. In high concepts of philosophy, the Indian Brahman sought salvation from the misery of life. All that knowledge has grown obsolete. It is no more wanted but as a curio. It is only as a curio that the so-called Eastern philosophy interest a savant here and a savant there in the enlightened universities of the West. The endless talk of the priest and the preacher after a brief flash-like instant of the live inspiration cause a just resentment in all healthy minds. All creeds of the popes and the priests are organized creeds of hatred. No truly religious mind can have the audacity to convert people, it would only help those who seek its help. When the zeal for preaching the doctrine is imported into the domain where ecstasy of the Pure must alone overpower the senses, the mischief starts. And world-wide mischief. Men fight like beasts for inflicting their religion on all others but themselves. So much so, that they wish to administer all human affairs under the religious codes of some laws based on bigotry and prejudice. Laws, that sentence saints of the other persuasion to death, are called 'divine religious laws'. And others issue other kind of mad dictates, numerous foolish do's and don'ts. One considers a particular diet religious and other irreligious. A Babel is created. Confusion worse confounded. Man dies like a drunkard, a hopeless fanatic without attaining any inner merit, all his life believing that he was over-religious.

When a system of religious thought begins to assert where man goes after death and how many millions of years he passes first in the moon and then in the sun, and that after all that celestial journey he is reborn on this wretched earth, surely, it can only interest rich idiots who have a good deal of time to waste on nothing. Imagine that if one, did not believe all this clotted nonsense, he was to be hanged for that. Wonderful 'religious' sense of law and justice! If dietary is not left to the science of medicine, religion invites just ridicule for meddling with affairs it cannot know as such. The latest Hindu reformer also turns on the same point as his ancestors did in thinking of a life of celibacy as a religion or a spiritual act. Surely, the secrets of organotherapy can be learnt in a laboratory better than from a so-called religious man.

2. The Farthest To-day

So all religions are dying. The old 'Divine Knowledge' is reduced to ashes like the terrible 'She'.

It is, however, very unfortunate that the to-day takes centuries for becoming the to-day for all. The majority of human beings live for ages in the dark of yesterday. The light of to-day takes its own time to reach the hearts of the people. Few get beyond these local darknesses. Animal humanity is in a long procession; the farthest end where the Light of Heaven beats upon it is much too far to be seen by all and the rear end forever receding is still in darkness! There are between the van end and the rear end a myriad viewpoints. And there are countless persons 'looking at their own navels' for Truth. It is wrong to say 'All paths lead unto Me'. All paths are at right angles to one straight path of human progress. They 'all lead away from Me'. For a universal compromise with the ignorant, it is an unprogressive saying that kills the individual impetus to go forward.

When you get to the real and the only right viewpoint of the latest, newest Dawn, that breaks on the farthest camel of this travelling caravan of humanity in this eternal procession, you will instinctively drop all other views. Just as when sleep over-powers you, your own hands drop from you, so when Truth comes to you, all other systems of things drop from you. Such is the symptom of a true religious and spiritual consciousness. Thus on any personal theme of this kind, there can be a myriad views and view-points for men who have not yet seen that Glory. For those who have seen, there is but one Path to Him. At the farthest end is the Light of Today and it is just born, new, fresh and to most of us it is but a distant vision. Almost a faith.

I see in the writings of the Sikh Gurus, the elimination of all wayside viewpoints of truth. All gods and goddesses have been dropped in *Akal Ustat* by Guru Gobind Singh. All religions and biases for man-made ethical systems have been dropped in the hymns of *Guru Grantha*. This casting off is at times so rapid that one feels that meteoric fire in the words of the Guru. See how Guru Nanak relinquishes the flat plains of the intermediate wayside view and touches the morning sun in *Asa di Var*. Guru Ram Das renounces all in One Name. So does, in his glorious and majestic chants, Guru Arjan Dev. It is a most remarkable phenomenon of soul-consciousness, that all so-called religious and philosophic systems are thus let go. Every system that called men to the knowledge of the Unknowable has been rejected, for the Guru is the Light and the Way. The whole of the old Brahmanical or ecclesiastical and theological atmosphere is destroyed as so much thick darkness in the Light of the Day. The classical cant and the priestly hypocrisy of renunciation, vows and celibacy, and all *Yogas* are put to the sword. The rattling tin-gods are thrown away. Such is *Guru Grantha*. And such is the theme of Guru Gobind Singh's *Akal Ustat*.

You would notice that whoever came to Guru Nanak had his viewpoint destroyed by his smile of the Infinite. And the new-corner was, in a winking, immersed in the oceans of the 'New Seal'. He became speechless, wonderstruck. He was lost in the Guru. All this came as a vision and as an action in dream, *in a smile, in a glance of the* Guru—Truly did Guru Nanak keep quiet. *That one live viewpoint cannot be given by word of mouth.* The word of mouth can only discuss from a million wayside intermediate viewpoints. As the seeker goes up the mountains to get a superview of the valleys below, so he realizes 'That' by seeing the Guru. Guru Nanak thus avoids being made the subject of an intellectual controversy like the *Brahman* of the Brahmans. He sinks the seeker into the depths of feeling, where all speech is hushed, and all thinking is full of revelations of the Beautiful. Guru Nanak himself is the religion of the disciple. What had Bhai Lehna found in Him? After seeing Him, his eyes were unwilling to open and see anyone else.

The devotion of Bhai Lehna to Guru Nanak is like the light of a kindled star. And Guru Amar Das never turns his back on Guru Angad Dev, but walks backward from Khadur to Goindwal. The other day, I saw a Sikh priest in fashionable cant, announcing to his audience in a lecture that he cannot turn his back on the Guru *Grantha*. Little did he know that Guru Amar Das has exhausted that particular feeling and- no more is left for any-one else to adopt. This wholeness of the intensity of a peerless love in an old man of seventy for his God, this revolving planet-like attraction of a man to author, is cosmic in its effulgence. The wooden peg which Guru Amar Das held, to stand and think of Him till the peg was worn out by his constant touch, is the emblem of his exquisite relish of His Remembrance. Lest the old body should drop, he propped it up to stand in the full effulgence of That Divine Presence. His religion is Guru Nanak. Spiritual attitude is a feeling that is born of the inspiration of the Guru. Nothing of man passes the Higher Realms of peace and love but this feeling, this spiritual attitude to the emancipated ones. Attitude is soul, it has no tongue, it is all senses concentrated in love towards

Him. As a dog leaps towards the Master, so the whole of the disciple is gathered in a dumb feeling for Him, the Guru. His lyrical glance keeps up this attitude. How many of us did find Him there when He was with us and how many now find Him when He is not with us. His being physically with us or not makes little difference. If they make of the religion of Guru Nanak a theological routine, they make of the starry sky a Lucknow clay-model. They only distress themselves by their smallness of vision and the misery of an utter bankruptcy of soul.

I tell you, unless we reject whatever we have made of ourselves and our religions we cannot be Sikhs, as He called us. Unless we are caught in the cosmic attractions of the Great planets of Guru-consciousness, unless we are thereby transmuted into angels, as it is written in *Asa di Var,* we cannot be His disciples. Guru Nanak is the only Truth in the glorious inspiration of the Sikhs. There is only one way to Him. And the way is found when He meets us, when He comes to us. And this one Truth is the vision of the *Guru Grantha*. After the long black night when we stand face to face in the effulgence of the Dawn that breaks from His forehead, we experience the very first sensation of religion. Those of us who have once experienced that ineffable glory, have entered the Path and they can be no more what they were. Their attitude has changed. They have become truly spiritual. What we do to rise up to it is our *Karma* and is of no consequence. What He sends down to us as His Love is truly spiritual. *Karma* is objective, it is at play in the objective world. His Grace is subjective, the only true spiritual substance of man. The spiritual reap crops they have never sown, it is a realm beyond our poor *Karma* and its deadly reckonings.

3. Spiritual Attitude

To what can I liken it, for it is an inspired state of self-consciousness. It is radiant, rich, self-centred in every individual's own subjective Universe of the Beautiful. Right here, in this very flesh and blood, it takes one out of it all and makes him live to his inward God-Love in as spontaneous a balance, as the lesser beings live effortlessly their lesser lives. But I might give a symbolic idea of that life freed absolutely from all earth and its grossness of body, mind and 'soul', by appealing to your own experience. On a soft spring morning, on a river bank, as one takes off one's clothes, leaving oneself to the kisses of the sun, to the soft touches of the sun-warmed sands, one feels so delightfully and so simply free of all clothes and concerns. So beautifully freed from the grossness of the earth, when immersed in the shining blue waters of a flowing river, one feels *truly* joyous. Of that joy, purity, innocence and virtue are mere shadows. The naked swimmers throw up their legs and hands and swim. They look at the sun and the sky, unconsciously being infinite. The spiritual attitude is of absolute freedom which comes to us all without fighting for it, without struggling for it.

> "The beards of the young men glistened with wet, it ran from their long hair,
> "Little streams passed all over their bodies,
> "An Unseen hand also passed over their bodies,
> "It descended trembling from their temples and ribs.
> "The young men float on their backs, their white bellies bulge to the sun, they do not ask who seizes fast to them,
> "They do not know who puffs and declines with pendant and bending arch,
> "They do not think whom they souse with spray."
>
> — *Walt Whitman*

True freedom is the spiritual state, the soul-consciousness. It is an attitude towards the world that seems outside and an inner attitude with which one lives in his real subjective

Universe, each separate infinite for each individual soul. And all other liberties are shadows of that inner attitude.

True knowledge is not knowing, but being. Knowing is always wrong, being is always tight. What I gather round me does not confine me. What I produce out of me does not exhaust me. Knowledge does not add anything to me. Ignorance does not diminish me. I come out of all my pursuits, as the bather comes out of his clothes. Coming out of thoughts, concerns, responsibilities, I enter into my real world.

This seeming, solid world, as it seems, is unreal; it is real as far as it coincides with my inner world. And the two worlds meet only in rare silver points where I cannot distinguish the inside from the outside. Every prosperity is the result of this union in an undetermined space of soul.

"O Something unproved, Something in a trance.
"To escape utterly from others' anchors and holds,
"To drive free, to love free, to dash reckless and dangerous,
"To court destruction with taunts and invitations,
"To ascend, to leap to the heavens of the love indicated to me.
"To rise thither with my inebriate soul,
"To be lost, if it must be so, "To feed the remainder of life with one hour of fullness and freedom,
"With one brief hour of madness and joy."

—*Walt Whitman*

4. NAM DEV

Nam Dev, an ecstatic person, sees what we do not see. His here is not here. With eyes like ours, all open, he sees inward. Nam Dev is going to the town where he imagines his Beloved lives. He calls it—Dwarka. The physical Universe all round him is only a Milky Way, to that Shining City. He is a pilgrim. His eyes see neither tight nor left; they are fixed on the vision of that Shining City of the Beloved.

While tramping for many days to Dwarka, Nam Dev got tired. By the way, these jewel-like men are not very much intended for this world. They live inwardly, invisible to the eyes of the earthly people, and seek no comforts for the body. They wear the body as a cloth. So clad in a stray cloth, alone, neglected, dust in his hair, he goes tramping on the road to the City of the Beloved. He just thinks how good it might be if he could get a mare to tide. It was a kind of prayer. A mare for the tired traveller—what a shining thought! No. This world is full of strange tyrants. Nam Dev suddenly sees a Pathan with long tresses wearing a huge splendid Afghan turban suddenly come out of nowhere, riding a fine blue mare and a foal behind. The Pathan, like the Englishman as anywhere to anyone in the oriental world, calls out imperiously to the tired saint. "Hullo! my foal is tired. Lift it up on your shoulder and follow me."

You see how the spiritual attitude lacks, what they call power to command, for it has chosen to obey. Nam Dev calls for a mare and gets one to carry. His feet are flat, his legs tired, but he must bear his cross. To such people, the renewal of their pain is the only relief they get from this world.

Were it I or you, we would begin to curse both God and man and cry in vain with Omar Khayyam:

> "An Love! Could I and thou with Fate conspire
> "To grasp the sorry scheme of things entire,
> "Shall we not shatter it to bits
> "And remould it nearer to the heart's desire?"

And neither Omar nor we shall ever feel ashamed of our foolish ignorance. What is the reply of Nam Dev to the great and wonderful response of Heaven to his prayer. He readily and gladsomely lifts up the foal on his shoulders and smiles askance and sings. With a little physical twitch, almost a shock, his mind mounts, his eyes lift up and he cries like a child with joy. Surely like the flower, the soul-consciousness of such men emits more perfume when hurt.

Nama's Song Ecstatic

In this Golden Land,
In the City of my Beloved,
Here in this *Dwarka* of God
In the beautiful world,
Is my Paradise,
Who can be an alien here?
How can there be any Moghuls in Dwarka?
The Moghul it cannot be,
It is He.
O Beloved!
How splendid is Thy Turban
How fatally sweet Thy speech,
Whence? O Whither? O Moghul! Whence?
Meeting me, O Beloved, so suddenly here, at this nowhere,
How kind of Thee, O Love!
What a delightful surprise!
O Love, O Love!

People think that omniscience and omnipotence are the qualities of a spiritual mind. In the lyrical colour of the soul-consciousness of Nama, such puerile virtues, all acquirable by certain processes of growth of man, are tinsel. One little 'jerk' of his consciousness puts him in the highest state of God-consciousness. All other virtues are mere darkness. Achievements but ashes.

In the Universe of Joy, there is nothing else real but He, the Personal Truth or The Bridegroom Glorious.

5. THE KING OF THE PURPLE COLOUR

Acute situations do arise, sometimes, in everyday human affairs when, the greatest of men have to call on Heaven's Glory for paltry things, as a bird might call to the high cloud and get a shower to wet his wings while flying in the full day's sunshine. Like the woodman in the fable, they do call even, at times, the Angel of Death and ask him to help them in putting a load of faggots on their heads. And what are those little things which get magnified by the lens of some local entanglement of one soul, say — curing of a patient, saving the honour of a protege, covering the fault of a beautiful large-hearted woman, protecting the honour and shame of a gentleman of faults, even asking forgiveness for a sin, and so forth? The day passes, and the dead yesterday becomes of no value in the expanses of Life; but while the day lasts, the last hour arrives, fates continue against the individual soul and the heroic man still stands fain by the sinner whatever his sin and by the needy whatever his need, because the nursing of a stray wound may be the only Truth available for that day, and the little microscopic act of mercy may be the only test of that Great Spiritual attitude. As said above, in these microscopic points might be the meeting of the inner and the outer universes and the irresistible functioning of soul-consciousness at such moments may be the only indication for a long time to come of the personal truth as manifested in the infinite number of the inner universes of Spiritual Beings. One of such spiritual prayers is that, for example, of Narsee. He lived under a straw-thatch, singing to himself. Perhaps he had a little shop where he earned his daily bread. As he was silent, they of his own called him mad and many a time played practical jokes on him. Once a pilgrim to Dwarka came to the city of Narsee and wanted to deposit his cash with a banker there for a draft on some correspondent of his in Dwarka. In those days, they were afraid of carrying cash with them and for the matter of that even now people are afraid to carry cash on their persons. Every banker in the city of Narsee referred the pilgrim to the shop of Narsee, and, though seemingly so poor, they said, he was the only one whose drafts could be honoured so far from there as Dwarka. It was all by way of joke, but the pilgrim would not take any denial from Narsee. Narsee, somewhat vexed and consequently aroused in some way, gone Out of his reverie, looked up to the pilgrim and smiled, "All right, I give you the draft. The name of my correspondent there at Dwarka is Sanval Shah — *King of the Purple Colour*. The pilgrim took the draft and went away to Dwarka. Narsee distributed all the wealth the pilgrim left with him to those who wanted it. Narsee had no use for it. This was an act of living faith. Narsee was on intimate terms with the *King of the Purple Colour*. In this personal intimacy lies all the secret of true spiritual inspiration and the maintenance of the right colour of spiritual vision. All spirituality is in finding Him and then not leaving Him. And all spiritual power is His coming to our aid. The pilgrim goes all the way to Dwarka where he searches for the banking house of the *King of the Purple Colour*. He finds not the *King of the Purple Colour*. No one knows Him. Disappointed and wholly broken in heart he comes out of the city of Dwarka. There is no such city on this earth. It is in the vision of the faithful. Such great cities are in the soul, nowhere outside us. Outside the city, in the open fields, he went wandering like an insane person and saying, "After all, that Narsee was a fraud". Poor recompense for all his loss was this uncharitable thought of Narsee. Further, under the mango trees he saw a simple black man who slowly came towards him and asked him what the matter was with him. The pilgrim gave his whole story. Whereupon the black man says to him, "I am the *King of the Purple Colour*" and counts out the cash to him and thus honours the draft of Narsee!

The pilgrim got his gold, but forgot that the *King of the Purple Colour* was a vision, not a reality in the sense of his gold, and yet the 'reality', so-called, was counted under the shadow of that mango tree, which very tree too disappeared the next moment!

6. The Jealous God

A poor Sikh retailer was once arrested in that wild savage Kabul, in those old days of Guru Har Rai, the Master of Amritsar. The charge against him, the shopkeeper, was that he weighed less. His particular weight was not up to the right legal standard. The law makers of Kabul were bent upon throwing the Sikh, the disciple of the Master, into the burning oven, for he was weighing less than the material needed for making bread. The law of Kabul had neither pity nor sympathy for him. But whatever his fault, his wife and daughter and children were all dependent upon him and they cried. He, if alone, could have endured any punishment, but seeing the piteous condition of his family, he too cried out to the Master. With all his faults, he had the unique distinction of being His disciple. The cry reaches the throne of Amritsar, for the Master is so close to his disciples. He hears the soft moaning of his children that went crying to sleep in the street dust of Kabul. He hears the soft sobs of a wife that lay fainting on the floor of her house at Kabul, crying to the Master, "Save him, pray, save him!" and so intensely that her cry stabbed her dead on the floor.

The Master sat at Amritsar. It is written that a devotee had just then come and offered five copper pice to Him. The Master did not notice the corner, but took his five pice and began, in a meaningless way, putting them now in his right, then in his left hand and went on doing this wayward act for a couple of hours or so. As he threw the pice down he said, "Thank God, My Sikh is saved."

And there in Kabul, at that very time, the balance was trembling in favour of the disciple. His weight was being tested, now on the right pan, then on the left. They found at last that the weight was quite accurate. It was certainly immaterial whether the man or his family was destroyed or not, but when the Man of Prayer chose to throw the weight of his faith into the balance for being weighed along with the disciple as a reality of the soul, and not as a mere illusion, like many things of the earth earthly, he was saved. The Response of the Guru is varied and, at all times, living. The mother covers all the faults of her child. As justice is tempered with mercy, so it is with the Guru, the Personal God of men. A thief no more remains a thief after having obtained faith and a thief, too, is bound to be saved when he, in some unknown strange kind of distress, calls upon Him for His Mercy in such an undetermined way that he himself does not know to repeat it in that way at another time. Prayers like this, too, are forms of inspiration.

7. KABIR AND HIS WIFE LOI

Kabir, now the Great Kabir on this earth, once lived here, persecuted by the Brahmins, earning his bread and supporting his wife and children by weaving cloth. His wife and daughter carded for him, his son set the loom and he wove. And all sang the joy of having met Him. Their substance of life was of the Heavens. Once, they say, a thief came in at the dead of night, hounded by the police. Kabir quietly put him alongside his own daughter and asked him to go to sleep. The police came and saw no stranger there. Here was Kabir, there his son, there his wife and yonder his daughter and his son-in-law! This was one small act of a truly spiritual person. And of his generosity, we hear in a folk song of Pothohar, still sung by the old ladies. I have heard it sung by my old mother-in-law, and my wife. The setting of the song is the occasion of a guest coming to Kabir and he having nothing to feed the guest with. The guest was a vision for Kabir. All household articles had already been sold or mortgaged, and only the previous day had Kabir pawned his sacred book. And that day there was nothing more in the house to be sold or pawned. This world does not lend money without security, though it receives unabashed so much of God's air and light and water and earth and sky, and the song of birds and the thrills of life for nothing.

> Kabir to his wife:
> > Loi, Loi, Loi!
> > We pawned our sacred book yesterday
> > And it is your turn to-day.
>
> Loi to Kabir:
> > Kabir, Kabir,
> > Yesterday as I passed through the market,
> > A Bania looked at me,
> > If I promised him a night,
> > I could serve the need of the house of your generosity.

The night came, Loi dressed herself to go to fulfil her engagement. But it began to rain heavily. Her poor dress would be spoiled. She would be wet. Kabir lifted her up on his shoulders and with a blanket thrown over her, he went and left her at the door of bania. The rain stopped as she arrived there. Kabir returned home. The night was dark. The streets muddy and Loi knocked at the door of the Bania.

Bania to Loi:
> Loi, Loi,
> It is pouring,
> The streets are muddy,
> And you arrive unwetted in the darkness of the night,
> How have you come, O Loi.

Loi to Bania:
> "Kabir lifted me on his shoulder,
> The Heaven put the umbrella on him,
> That is how I came, O Bania,
> Though the night is dark,
> The streets are muddy,
> I came with my God with me.

Bania *falls at her feet and cries:*
> "As Kamal is Thy son, O Mother,
> So take me as one,
> Thy crying child, Mother,
> O Mother, how ablaze with lustre are these shining raiments of thine,
> Mercy! Mercy! Mercy!

These great lovers like Kabir have an infinite spirit of spiritual enterprise, for they have truly seen Him. They know Him and He has promised His eternal friendship to them!

8. LORD GAURANGA

And you have heard of Chaitanya—the white Lord Gauranga of black Bengal. He threw his ass-loads of books on logic into the Ganges and became suddenly mad with the joy of having met Him, as did Nam Dev when he met the Moghul. It might have been this time, in the place of the Moghul, the tender trembling of the leaf or the passionate heaving of the branches of the woods in the moonlight, in which strange quivering of delight the inner God might have manifested Himself to him. Thenceforward, he was more than the moon that shone on the sea. There was the lustre of the Strange Man he met in the woods, radiating from Chaitanya. And his madness became deeper, he was lost here and found there. He went, it is written, to a Hindu temple where thousands of votaries went to worship the stone effigy of Krishna. Seeing his Beloved in the disreputable form of a black stone-idol badly carved, Chaitanya flew into a frenzy. He went straight up to the pedestal, caught hold of the black idol and threw it out of the shrine and sat in its place for days and nights like a statue, as in Europe, they tell us, once stood Swedenborg, rapturous of his celestial visions.

Then the ruling Moghuls of Bengal ruled, "Stop him from singing. He disturbs our sleep and the comfort of our Harems!" The summons went to Chaitanya. That very night, it is said, he walked straight into their private Harems and kept up his choir of divine singing till the small hours of the dawn, transfixing the Moghuls and their ladies in one continuous divine rapture.

Has not sincerity its way open in all directions and unto all hearts?

He went across the river in another frenzy of old friendship and beat his scholar friend and drove out, with his fists, the foolish scholarship out of his bones. For when the Pandit friend of his came to his senses, he had renounced the philosophy of Vedanta and realized his friend Chaitanya as his religion.

9. An unknown Sikh saint who cultivated his lands

A Sikh peasant of the Punjab did plough but he belonged wholly to the Guru's song. Like a bird on the *Kikar* branch, he sang 'Guru Nanak, Guru Nanak' he piped. The practical men of affairs asked him why he kept on so continuously troubling himself with calling Guru Nanak, when they never saw the Guru come to Him! "Brothers," said the boor, "I am not well. I feel a pain in my very pores. Every hair of mine pricks me in the skin as if it were a needle. Every pore aches. I feel so feverish with the pain. When I call upon the Guru, I feel soothed, cooled. His name cools me. When I say not, I feel great heat tearing me. I return to the Name again and again, for it is my only comfort."

And what had he developed into by this simple aching for Him? A dumb inarticulate spiritual attitude to God, the Beloved!

The Guru has told us that this dumb attitude is the absolute spirituality. It is the aching love for Him.

10. The Music of Universal Fellowship

All these people had the deep spiritual attitude.

You will naturally ask me of what use are such men? Useful men are stale, smelling of age-long putrefaction; nothing noticeable, nothing remarkable. Dead rotten fuel!

It is these beautiful men of the true spiritual attitude who are of no use to you in your sense, that are the salt of the earth and belong to the domain of that superior class of that un-understandable spiritual genius. Their potential power, so cosmic in its quality, is beyond our comprehension and computation. They cannot weigh to you what you want, but they give you what you do not require now, and which will be your only sustenance a little hereafter and forever.

You remember that story that Carlyle repeated in his speech at the memorial meeting held in memory of Goethe in Germany. All wise men of the Church too had come to honour the poet and artist and in their learned encomiums bestowed upon Goethe, they wished he were but a little more Christian than artist and a source of great inspiration and help to their Church. And Carlyle made them all writhe under his just sarcasm. "Gentlemen," said Carlyle, when he got up arranging his spectacles on his nose, and looking obliquely in the direction of the glorious lights of the Church; "You remember the story of that idiot who had come out one fine morning, with a cigar in his mouth, calling upon the sun to come and light it for him. And you remember how he cursed the sun because he Would not come down to him and light his cigar!"

Useful men, good men! Tons of them! Pshaw! They have no spiritual character in spite of a thousand principles and vows and vigils and high moral concepts. Amorphous powder of dust that flies in common streets!

The so-called ethical and religious systems of this world of uninspired 'thinkers', like those luminaries of the wiseacrely Church that had gathered to do honour to Goethe, are empty of the essence of the true spiritual attitude.

A music of universal fellowship sounds yonder and the bathers in the Dawn In the sky are entranced! They have renounced their bodies in the trance of the Ineffable, and, behold! they are not drowned.

> They have jumped into the river, the river is in flood,
> You, too, O delicate Maiden Beautiful!
> Jump, dare, jump!
> For on the other shore is the Beloved.
> Behold! His arms are spread,
> Is not He forever gathering you to Himself?
> Jump, O Beautiful Shy Maiden! Jump.
> And the maiden did jump,
> Hush; her song of love still sounds in their inner Universe.
> O Mother! hold me not,
> Forbid me not from that Door of Light,
> These your palaces are a curse,
> Forbid me not from seeking Him!
> The king sends the poison cup,
> To kill Mira,
> Mira drinks it as the cup of nectar,
> The king sends the black cobra to bite Mira.
> Mira is safe, the cobra bites her not!

11. 'BREAD', 'WOMAN' AND 'BRIDEGROOM'

These three words are used here in a special symbolic sense. Bread *for the physical needs of man, the animal;* Woman *for beauty, the mental need of man,—of the intellectual halfman on the way to self-realization;* Bridegroom *for the Guru or Personal God, the spiritual need of man,—of the angel whose two wings of flight are the mind and the body.*

Man the animal, cannot live without Bread. Man, the mind, cannot be without Woman. And man, the soul, is dead without the Guru. His hunger makes all the subjective worlds objective. His passion makes all the objective worlds wholly subjective. His ever rising aspirations for the Highest are fulfilled by finding Him, the Guru, the God. Bread ceases to be reality where Woman' becomes reality and 'Woman' ceases to be reality where 'Guru' becomes it. When the 'Gum' Informs man's both Woman' and 'Bread' the man has entered the path of discipleship and his attitude has regained its lost Spiritual Balance.

(A) BREAD

The beautiful dove must needs eat worms. Her spiritual eyes shine because of the worms she has been picking up the whole day. And the spiritual aspirations of man help him to transcend the body and its requirements. To have less of bread shows celestial taste. To appropriate as little as possible of this physical world is, therefore, a moral act. In that sense, Alexander, Nadir Shah, Changez Khan and Napoleon are like the non-moral catastrophes of Nature, red in tooth and claw, while Kanad who lived on the stray pickings out of the harvested rice fields of Bengal is truly a man ascending some way to spiritual vision.

The politics of the world of hunger for the physical are of the monkey who came to divide the bread equally between a cat and a dog, and, with the balance in hand, to give nothing to the litigants but to cut out a larger piece again for himself from the bigger slice as still not balancing. All political intrigues, including those of commerce, manufacture and other so-called economic problems, are stories of the tiger lying in ambush.

The spiritual attitude in this world of hunger is, what Mr. Henry Ford says work, labour and sweat and forget the physical world. The only possible transcendence from it is through work. In this 'space' of Bread, overwork to death or starve to death; there is no other alternative, it seems. The habit of working for work's sake is the foundation on which the ideal state can be founded. The old Brahmin was certainly well-fed and well-looked after when he wished to transcend this hard world of bread through speculative philosophy!! As a matter of fact, all nations of men, like flocks of crows, are confusing all other issues for the sake of bread.

They are, therefore, fictitious types of men who speculatively deny 'Bread'. It is remarkable that the Gurus tell us that if your spiritual attitude is right, then 'blessed is your festive board'. Think of Him while chewing life out of the wheaten bread for yourself, 'blessed are your horses going laden with merchandise'.

And if by eating, your mind is rotated wrongly, that eating is poisonous for you;
And if by wearing, your mind is rotated wrongly that wearing is poisonous for you.
And unless you labour and sweat and earn your Bread, all other crusts are full of poison for you.

For centuries in morbid India, such healthy views were never so boldly given to the people whom metaphysical inanities and Yogic abnormalities oppressed into abject slavery.

It shall be at once admitted that the bread problem of man should be solved on a large scale according to the moral law within the soul-consciousness of man. And that undetermined Ideal State is yet to come into being, where all the optimum physical needs of man necessary to keep the soul-plant of man in vigorous growth are equitably provided. It cannot be done in a day. But the direction of all politics must be towards equal distribution of comforts and needs in a spirit of loving comradeship. The Guru demonstrated this once in history. How? They established such a democracy with the divine Aristocrat, the Beloved of all, full of deep and spiritual self-renunciation, in the centre. It was no democracy in the modern political sense of Government by votes. It was democracy by obedience to Him. All equally obeyed the Great Will. All lost themselves in Love; no one asserted his little i-ness. All dissolved themselves in Him and out of Him came out as new men. Without the Guru this democracy cannot be maintained. And if Mussolini and Kamal Pasha have, in the teeth of democracies, stood high as aristocrats, they only go to prove the efficacy of the method of the Sikh Gurus in their endeavours to establish an Ideal State. They are yet below that standard of individuality which the Guru invoked for the establishment of the Ideal State. The requisite renunciation of the individual in dedication to society or state can only come when the state is identified with the Beloved. This is the Khalsa scheme of the world governance of *Bread* and *Woman*. Love of the Beautiful Beloved has in it the genius of new social reconstruction. *The politics of the Sikh, therefore, are but the gladsome, spontaneous renunciation of the little self in the love of the Guru; and while living in that sacred vision he labours and distributes the fruits of his labour on the roadside, almost subconsciously.* He lives elevated above the sordid details of right and might, for he has found better occupation in his love. Like trees, he drives his struggles below the ground and his blossoms and fruits up into the air. Death to him is as welcome. Not the great renunciation, but the small joys of continuous self-sacrifice, at every step, at every breath. In this sense of self-sacrifice alone, to contribute one's mite to the coming of the Kingdom of Heaven within man, as Jesus Christ put it, is the Sikh, or the Disciple of the Guru, to enter into the activities of the state. Unless the rich atmosphere of peace is brought in, where the tiger and the lamb drink at the same pool, there can come no true culture in the *bread-affairs* of man. The *bread-affairs* engross all political activity of man, and the true progress of man is to make it so simple as the provision of sunlight by the sun. The state needs to be organized on the rich love of man to man.

Bread is a grim reality, then, which, at times, shatters all beautiful visions, but while in that savage struggle, we, as the disciples of the Truth-embodied, the Guru, should not forget that it is transcendence above the body and its needs that is the ultimate satisfaction of bodily desires. By it, we have to rise above it. Work makes us spiritual. Let us therefore give up all other worship of God but work. This is the fundamental message of the Guru to the man in struggle, to the man bound in body. The worker, the labourer is the man of honour; the creator of bread is *man in spiritual action.*

These *spiritual politics* of the Guru have been interpreted by the modern book-reader as Bolshevism. Bolshevism is a great upheaval and an experiment. But as it is about the body, it cannot triumph. The selfishness of man cannot be got rid of by small men like Lenin and Trotsky. Tolstoy tried without success to introduce some vague spiritual aim in Russian Politics, but without the *Beautiful Autocrat in the centre,* the whole frame was bound to collapse. The Terror created by the Russian Council could not replace the King. The bad Kings are very bad, so are Lenins. The true King seated in every heart and the true King on the throne of the State is certainly the end of all Bolshevik protests, but are they informed of the Guru?

You merely as an academic person have to consider dispassionately some aspects of such political upheavals in the world as expression of some divine secret of geological sort of social changes. The modem socialist and his extreme type, the Bolshevist, condemn capitalism. It is certainly condemnable from the standpoint of the poor. Someone gets rich with a palace and a queen, and the other one with similar features starves with his wife to death. As much a queen, the poor man's wife: as much the prince and the princess, the poor man's son and daughter; but the latter in a way, are eternally bereft. It is terrible to contemplate how men neglect men. But have they become men? Now when they shall become men, all shall be men; none will be bereft at least of an ample provision for bread and clothes and huts and life's joys that such things provide. And they do provide. I saw my bullock and my horse doing nothing but eating all the twenty-four hours. Miserable would I be if I were to eat all the day long, but I too meet my fellowmen and women best at the dinner table. There is a joy spiritual in sitting to breakfast and dinner and tea together, as we are very much animals still. The more we subordinate the physical life to the intellectual and the intellectual to the institutional and spiritual, the more we ascend to God.

After *Bread* or *Physical Body* comes the civilization of the intellectual man. What *Bread* is to the body, *Woman,* a symbolic name for culture, and its needs, is to the refined intellect.

There is the divine glow of a refined intellect of an elevated mind which feels disgusted with the mud and squalor of the poor. There is that iridescent, artistic beauty of well-fed society, the brilliance of the sweet-mouthed, well-dressed, women in their bejewelled palaces; and, in all such aristocratic things of joy created by the king and the palace, there is an expression of beauty which lures the human mind again and again to attain these artificial splendours and those gem-like glories. There, in the palaces, woman's beauty is almost made celestial, she is full of graces that cannot possibly be seen anywhere else. Without riches there would have been no such artistic expressions as *the woman of the palace,* nor things like the Cross of Notre Dame and the great cathedrals of Europe.

Poor men build, paint, and model in obscurity and the best of the rich men make them available as light of the world. The aristocracy is the publisher of all art. The Roman Church and its building, its painted walls and its pictures, are due to wealth. The great cities of Europe like Venice, are built by its rich merchants. Those great treasures of art which Ruskin loves to describe in aristocratic words and thereby creates meanings and delicate shades of significance in the stones and sculpture of Europe are due to the same rich instinct of men.

Buddha would have died unnoticed but for the Empire and the mind of Ashoka to publish Buddhism. Wealth, material prosperity or symbolically in one word *Bread,* is thus a reality not only to be reckoned with, but to be respected and honoured in some good sense in which creative poverty with an aristocratic mind and word and thought is to be honoured and respected. Truth needs a myriad forms. A man who is successful in his small blind way has some worth in him; it is not to be talked away as something ignoble. In certain phases of human life, perhaps the greatest thing is this material wealth when it becomes through the great spirit of a genius, the vehicle of the highest Truth, the soul. Carlyle, in his 'Cromwell as a Hero', almost comes to the identity of the body and the soul. It is in this sense, that aristocracy is after all, with all its sins, as bad or as wrong as democracy. The rich man is as much a medium of the expression of nature's hidden purposes as the poor. So the great seers, unlike the Bolshevist and the socialist, do not rush to seek a solution of this problem in the destruction of the rich as a class, for the rich are as worthy of their pity as the poor. Largeness of vision in such matters is the cure of the disease of wrong emphasis on the oblique forms of the views of man. It is the spirit of his views which will be found identical both in aristocracy and democracy. They are both good when good, bad when bad, the latter hopelessly so always. There is no doubt that the French Revolution and the Russian Revolution are like tornado blasts to show how much the idle capitalists oppress the workmen. And the direction of all politics is to be to aid the man who works, for he truly loves also. No self-government of the people, by the people, for the people can be a substitute for the enlightened state with its direction towards the uplift of the man who works and loves, who weaves and aches for the inaccessible beauty of the stars. There is no such thing as Swa-raj, self-government; we are always governed best by a noble man, not by ourselves if we are not so noble. The rest are mere words, votes, democracy. All honour therefore to those humanitarian statesmen imbued with the far-seeing spirit of true altruistic statesmanship, who are engaged as labourers of love insetting the *Bread* affairs of man in the spirit of equal distribution of *Bread.*

(B)   WOMAN

Next to *bread,* the essential man is centred in his divine love for *woman.* His sexless passion also has *woman* as its *terra firma.* All his glorious hopes and aspirations are bees humming round this *flower—woman.* The Home of Love revolves round her as a dream beauty. In a great and cultured world, the honour for woman must needs be infinite. I do not think that the ideal honour for woman is as yet in sight. As George Meredith puts in the mouth of Bis Diana of the Crossways, "Men may have rounded *Seraglio Point,* they have not yet doubled *Cape Turk."*

Woman shall be the second best God or the God of the intellectuals on earth. She shall be absolutely free. And it is out of her freedom that we shall yet win new ideals of Home and Art. I tell you as a beloved slave of man she has contributed a major portion of the whole of his culture and civilization. The slavery of woman to man is due to man largely but essentially to the woman herself. Only in motherhood does she become free. A divine sovereignty is then conferred on her. Her intuitive omniscience is more developed than man's. Her spirit of self-sacrifice is real and mans is more or less dramatic and unreal.

The whole of *Guru Grantha* is the voice of a wedded woman or a maiden pining in love of the Beautiful. Her nobleness in *Guru Grantha* is infinite, her freedom is of the highest. Both man and woman as sexes are forgotten in her voice. She becomes the Supreme Reality and a freed Soul. In the freed soul alone is the subordination of one to the other effectively abolished and all disputes hushed.

As Bolshevism is in modern politics so is the modern women's movement in the sphere of woman; both are protests. There is something rotten in the systems of our marriages and social inequalities and the protest is to bring better culture. Much is frivolous futility in such ill-balanced movements. But the balance shall tremble again and woman shall find her real spiritual worth in herself. So far she is still a toy-like thing. In her imagined freedom what is she doing? Aping man. Man himself is yet in his swaddling clothes. Let us look at the modern woman a little and compare that old and this new. She has certainly lost her beauty and has not yet gained her soul. When in that old superb figure of hers the Christ-Braids fell all about her swanlike neck, her face shone in this world like the moon in black clouds. Even that so-called savage Afridi of the Indian Frontier was moved to sing of "the *bazar* of the tresses of my Beloved", and in passionate worship of her the most brutal of men found some kind of cultural atmosphere. It was the culture of total self-sacrifice for her sake. In her worship too is all patriotism, honour of a race, war and defence of home and hearth. What would freedom itself be if man were devoid of woman worship? One wonders what is woman. Man called her wife, but she stood as his daughter before him and she made a Buddha of her father. She was always a mystery to the human race. Her tresses suggested a secret, her eyes that loved made it deeper. The virgin was desired by the young man, he fell worshipping before her, she was the mother and he the son. Her clothes were a Universe in themselves and her soul was sought after from eternity to eternity. It was hidden in the fold of her clothes, it was fluttering of someone's heart in the flapping of her veil-cloth. The national flags are dim shadows of the veil-cloth that flies, as the sister of the nation runs appealing to man—"up and fight, for I am in danger." The other day the eastern wind was flaunting a sun-lit cloud before my eyes. I thought it was the veil-cloth of my mother, and I stood up thinking my mother had come back from the dead. I shed a tear and the sun went past me. The woman's forehead we have for centuries contemplated as our sky aglow with the calm sparkle of the moon. Poets sang and husbands and fathers and all poets in action in this living love of woman, died serving her and her children.

The mother mysterious, so noble, divine, so full of love that she drew the whole-souled devotion of humane men for centuries and was still a mystery. She was as mysterious as Nature. A literature was born, an art became alive, a history was made glorious in the defence of her honour and pride. Woman was still a mystery. And for ever concealed was her face in the night of her hair, in the mystery of her clothes, in the appeal of her eyes and in the music of her voice and she was revealed partly to man in her acts of faith, love and noble self-sacrifice. She wore the cross of the whole family as did Jesus, but started no Christianity. Every woman is the Messiah. Her daily life in the service of man gave us the songs of her beautiful soul as the shifting colours of the sky and the changing lines of Nature tell us of Nature's inner Person.

Woman was thus the inspiration for all the heroic efforts of man to make himself man. Woman is responsible for all his best longings for immortality, for all his religions, for all his arts, and for all his noble wingings above earth and sky. And when I contemplate the modem type of woman that has denuded her head of hair and her limbs of the mystery of clothes and when she has not, by throwing all these cumbersome veils aside, revealed her soul to us, I fall dead with despair—whither is she going? The world has become emptied of human beauty. I wanted to cling to her soul, the immortal portion of her, and she wishes me to cling to her flesh and bone which is precious only because of her great soul. Otherwise all is mutton, mere mutton. None need quarrel with her experiments with herself. Of course she is absolutely free to do as she chooses, but we are concerned in the decoration of the Temple of flesh where we have worshipped for so many centuries and poured out our soul. And when someone asked me what is the Ideal of modem Art. I replied "speed". Get into a motor car, free of all encumbrances. Speed! more speed! Bang! Dash against the mountain! And to pieces! There lie the mutton pieces! The end! Discovered! Man a corpse! Woman a corpse! To come to such a discovery is the suicide of all civilization.

In this too, the Guru leads the ideas of the coming world. If Sikhs of to-day there are who veil their women and enslave them, they are not of the Gurus. The third Guru while giving audience to a Hindu Queen of Mandi when she came all veiled to Him said, "You O mad woman, have come to see the Guru and you cover your face from Him." How can those who call themselves His disciples tolerate anything infringing the absolute freedom of woman. On the other hand, those who free her and ape the Western fashions remind one, as Marie Corelli graphically puts it, "of the poultry yard." That is certainly worse than nursing a peculiar type of womanhood of noble self-restraint behind the oriental veils. Veils often symbolise the beauty and mystery of the concealed and the veiled is more sacred than the unveiled. But if veils accentuate this sex difference or unveiling does the same, both are Unholy. Only when man and woman both live above body and mind as freed souls, they represent the culture of live freedom. Live freedom is freed also of sex differences. Stupid, indeed, are those sects who wish to get rid of woman as an obstacle to spiritual progress. Woman is the greatest and truest aid to the maintenance of the true spiritual attitude. Woman's soul crying to the soul of man is the only divine lyric trembling like the music of the Infinite and the Eternal. Man's self-transcendence is as much of him, as his physical indulgence, as his Intellectual aestheticism. He is a spirit. It is when the spirit of the Holy Ghost fills him and his body and *bread,* his intellect and his *woman* are suffused with his discovery of the personal God in man and Nature that Man, the artist becomes himself the highest Art—the expression of the mystery of life. The true artist is the best art, the best culture, the best literature and the best religion.

(C) THE GURU OR THE DIVINE BRIDEGROOM

Meeting Him, the Guru, the Personal God, is a whole spiritual enlightenment in a glance. It is the sudden discovery of one's highest and utmost self. He is the ultimate Reality of the subjective universe within me and also without me. Without Him, it is all dark. Dante's Heavens are lighted by the figure of his Beatrice. The Guru's presence is like the coming into our soul of the whole spiritual universe peopled with shining gods and angels. All that is, is true in the Guru, with the Guru. Without Him, all gods and angels are ghosts of darkness.

Our descriptions of the higher unseen universe of our soul may be right or wrong, but there would be no higher aspirations, burning in the bosom of man, no 'Godward tendency' in life, if we cease to be after death. 'The rose that blows for ever dies', is a pleasant blasphemy. And so are the guesses of like nature that life is but a diseased condition of matter, and so forth.

If it were so, the glint of the stars, the glow of the maiden's cheek, the delightful promise of soul in the companionship of man and Nature would never be so mysteriously fascinating. Even if we cannot prove it, a blind belief in this great Unseen is a wonderful justification of our being. The true spiritual power comes to man from this inner universe. Imagination gives wings to man to fly thither. All knowledge is inspiration. Man's spiritual consciousness is in the keeping of those shining angels. They help him, as he falters on the path, they raise him to their holy bosoms. They kiss him when the friends of the world desert him. They protect his honour, they make him, if need be, great, supernatural, miraculous and wonderful, a genius in a moment. They do his biddings — even what he, like a child, may lisp unknowingly. The secret of his occasional omniscience and omnipotence are they who stand behind him. The Heavens run to stand at his back. His look upward draws all the gods together to aid him. Such a babe, almost an orphan, is powerful with the power of Heaven. He is not of his small will, but of the will of a whole inner universe. He is the perfect child and the perfect man who is so informed.

The Guru says, "Give to the child whatever he wants. Let the milk of love flow to him." Such a child sees him, drinks Him and swallows Him. To such a man all is beautiful. He sees beauty 'raining everywhere', beauty flowing in a thousand Ganges Out of him and engulfing the whole world in the vision of the Guru.

Thus, to the Guru's mind, man is normally and frankly physical, transcending which he is purely intellectual, brilliant, creative, artistic, aesthetic. Transcending all this intellectual self of his he is mostly intuitional, spiritual. And the highest type is he who has body and mind as mere shadows left, using them as mere instruments, tools or energies of his. And he is the one who, above all, has the illumined soul with its revolving Universe, with the Guru in the centre and shining in him is that wonder-woven starry Universe of his own individual, separate, beautiful subjective world of gods. He is always, in a splendid peace of sublimated passion. Those who, in their minds, even think of a greater God than the Guru, do not know what personal passion for the personal God is. And also they do not know that, as before death in this Dark world, so after death in the Bright world, there is essential need of personal friendship, its personal love and protection. Man is exactly in the same essential need of the assonance of soul to live here as well as hereafter. To speak a bit physically in a symbolic way, as ghosts roam here in the streets of London and New York and Lahore and Calcutta, so do they roam there; and the soul after giving up the body is in need of peace and comfort and safety, actual real comfort that true divine friendship provides. Just as the empty speculative talks or intellectual realizations that all is one, do not help anyone here, when the tyrant lays his hands on the innocent or when the animal with its paws jumps to capture a woman, so will they not be of any avail there. The Ghosts of Darkness waylay the traveller there and the association with the Angels of Light here through *Simrin* and *Nam* or divine friendship with the Great Masters, is a whole armour that gives the soul its victory after death. And so in daily life on this earth. All this psychic phraseology is only symbolic; it does not represent what actually takes place.

For the bee the lotus, nothing beyond; for the man the woman he loves nothing beyond; for the hungry the loaf of bread, nothing beyond; for the thirsty a cup of water, nothing beyond. Or why does sleep round up this little life? There is nothing beyond Buddha, Guru Nanak and Jesus Christ, for the little faith of man. And if there is, it is a trance of wonder, it is a slumber of ecstasy, it is death of self in love. It is ignorance of all else but Him. This is discipleship of that great spiritual attitude of man which comes to him as the great gift of the Creator.

The spiritual attitude is a live passion though dumb and inarticulate like that of the dog for his master. It is as much an act of creation as the solar system — we can make candles, not skins.

"I sing of Guru Nanak. I believe because Guru Nanak bids me", says Bhai Vir Singh, the disciple; "I do not sing Him whom sings the *Guru Grantha*, I sing only the Guru."

III

THE GARDEN OF SIMRIN

1. 'THE NAME'

Guru Nanak is 'the Name' we sing as the birds sing the joy of the new dawn. Guru Nanak, Guru Nanak, we say and we pass on. We look neither to the left nor to the right, with our lips sealed with honey of the Name, with our eyes enraptured by the dream of a greater, nobler universe of the Guru's mind. We go muttering even mechanically our *life-mantram* and we pass undisturbed and undisturbing into the heart of men and things. We go mingling like a good thought in the blood of the universe, 'the Name! the Name!'

As the babe knows its mother and nothing beyond, we know our Name and nothing beyond. They ask a mere child, what is, God and where? How could the little babe talk? The baby laughs. The babe hath not yet learnt language, nor thought. Do you believe in God or do you not? What impertinent questions are these and those. Enough, under the garment of the Guru I am concealed and blessed in my joy that knows no answer to these questions.

So you cannot fight the battles. You are seeking the peace of the soul without a body. And what is soul without the body. No, I have a Friend Divine that saves me and saves all. If I am to be I shall be of His Command and He knows more than you and I. I believe He makes His servant manifest in a day, in a moment. Greatness is all His. Great men are but mediums of His inspiration. He who is filled with the will of the Father is great. None else, none else. Greatness is of the service He gives to His servant to do. The bird on the bough that chirps a nascent note of morn is a hero to that extent. We believe that man is as powerless as the babe, as the calf, as the bird.

2. OUR LONG TRESSES

Don't you know these tresses of ours are the wandering waves of the sea of Illusion? Guru Gobind Singh gathered the waves of the Ocean of Consciousness as the mother gathers the hair of the child. What is man but an ocean of consciousness. The master washed them, combed them and bound them in a knot as the vow of the future manhood which shall know no caste, no distinction between man and man, and which shall work for the peace and amity of spiritual brotherhood. He who wears His knot of hair is a brother to all men, freed of all ill-feeling of selfishness. He is to be on the bayonet's point to be of no separatist creed, no religion, nor of any national combine of men bent upon loot and plunder and the tyranny of subjugating other men.

Those who do not yet understand the law of love cannot and should not wear the Master's knot of the sacred tresses and those who do should wear it as a token of spiritual isolation from the herd. So did Guru Gobind Singh command. And obedience to him is life. There is no life outside that Great Love.

The aim of the *Brothers of the tress-knot* of Guru Gobind Singh is different, different the direction, different their persuation.

We do not concern ourselves with the conditions of life. We glow like flowers on the thorny bed or on the bed of velvet moss with equal joy, for facing Him and living in Him and breathing Him is our life. And all who desire to be *Brothers of the tress-knot* of Guru Gobind Singh come and *be*. This is the life of love, not of any other truth. All other truths are of no concern to us! We are now the *Sangha* of the tress-knot of Guru Gobind Singh, our purposes are as inscrutable as those of the God of Destiny.

3. The Agitated Doves

Our Guru Nanak called men to the true instinctive goodness of man. He persuaded no one outside his centre of life. But he pitied man for not glowing up whatever he is and in whatever position he be. Conditions of life both of body and mind do not matter. A starved body and a well-cared-for one are of the same spiritual outlook. The joy of being His is independent of the highest intellectual richness or of the lowest poverty of intellect; the knowledge of the joy of soul is for ever independent. It is the life in full glow that the Guru kindles with his breath. Born in India, his language is limited to words in use here. He met both Moslems and Hindus and asked them to be men. Suggestions given for a new social reconstruction of the world on the law of love have been the Guru's contribution to the development of men. He created an ideal Society in Love of the Guru, — this was a great and successful experiment. Men, men, men; that is the call. It comes with the vigour and freshness of a new religion, no new sect but a powerful and sweet and unceasing call to man to his real and genuine manhood.

The tree that gives shade, the flower that gives fragrance even to the man with the axe, even to the crusher, has always understood the Guru better than men who very soon degenerate by the contagion of animal selfishness.

The full-blown lotuses, the full-blown roses, are alive with that spark of soul-sensitive life which the Guru says is spiritual; and not men with their diverse creeds and religions, and expanded and stuffed intellects. Of what use is that progress of man which does not make of him a brother to man and nature? Infinite sensitiveness of human or divine sympathy is life. But all our existing systems of ethics and religions and societies tend to make stones of us.

A troupe of doves, agitated doves, their white wings fluttering like the little dawn-lit clouds, by the joy of it all, is the symbol of the Guru's spirituality, not a stone image, nor age-smoothed pebble good.

4. Of Equal Dignity with the Stars

Spiritual attitude independent of the more or less 'evolved' stages of life, the dumb doe and the withered grass pray equally with the beautiful pheasant crying to the dawn with joy and the prophet in salutation to His God. It is the right axial standing up of a little fibre in the earth in equal dignity with the stars.

At one end superstition strikes at times unawares at the spiritual truth and at the other the highest enlightenment of a Buddha. The discussion about it and about the two poles is like churning water to skim butter, as if it were milk.

Asoka hungered for spiritual light after a whole age of ignorant conquests of empires. He turned poor. Why build an empire that has no moral value in the discovery of one's own soul?

5. The Guru-Personality Impersonal makes the Sangha

Nature makes individuals. They are as God made them, good, bad or indifferent. Pots, well-shaped or ill-shaped. As the Guru says some are cottonwooled in sweet languor, some are ever boiling kettles on fire, some full of cold water. All as Nature made them. They are as many flowers and leaves; and some are poisons, some are nectars. And the Guru Personality creates the people, the galaxy of God-intoxicated men, the *Sangha,* the *Sangat.* As the planets revolve round the central sun, so the people" new-born, faith-born, spirit-born, Guru-born, revolve round the Guru. This planetary constellation of living, song-like men, living musical presences, almost emitting the music of the very spheres, is the society of Remembrance, *Simrin,* of the Beautiful. Such are the disciple saints of *Simrin.* The earth tries to run away from the sun, but it is the sun that holds it on. The disciple is under the centrifugal forces of individuality, the Guru holds him under these centripetal forces Himward. This inspiration of *Simrin* is not of the individual, but of the cosmos. *Simrin* is always cosmic. The Guru's universal brotherhood is salvation from the selfishness of the inner forces that tend towards individuality.

Bhai Gurdas, the Apostle of the Guru's faith, says that it is Guru Nanak who opened the long-closed portals of true spiritual comradeship and taught people to surrender to fall at the feet of Brothers. The bowing down of the disciple is not' the symbol of any humility, but, it is the cosmic surrender of the individuality, however lofty and beautiful in itself, to the Guru-born society. One star gets bound in a cosmic unity. Individual opinions, vows, principles, emphasis on kings and cabbages, angularities, idiosyncrasies of men and animals have to be relinquished in the presence of the Brothers, as one renounces his very hands and feet when sleep overpowers him. Unless it is as spontaneous and easy, it has not that cosmic significance which the Guru attaches to it. Forced surrender or trained surrender has no meaning. Surrender has to be complete, unconditional, gladsome and spontaneous, and easy and simple. Conviction is of the depths of life; intellectual assent or critical appreciation has no substance.

Unless you are admitted into His acceptance there is no invitation for you into this Brotherhood. The Brothers help, but they do not insist on your joining it. Preaching is idle unless you have learnt the divine necessity of your soul, through the vicissitudes of life. If you develop that Asoka's thirst, the Brothers have a cup of nectar for you. They raise it to your lips. Truth is simple. Drink and you shall know of it. There is no conversion, except that loud and silent colour of life that suffuses you, deluges you, when you have drunk of the Nectar-cup of the Brothers.

How good is the Brother! When he speaks, a stream of vitalising honey flows out of his soul. He fertilizes many centuries with simple, sweet words. All make conditions and terms for proffering me their love, the Brother gives without asking even my name, as the river gives itself to bird, beast and man.

The Brother just looked at me as I was passing. And my bashful eyes looked from under the dropping eye-lids; he had closed his eyes and was praying for me. I never forget that sight. Whenever I am in a difficulty now, I close my eyes and see the Brother standing by my side in exactly the same posture and light radiates all around him. And that radiance envelops me and I forget the world. Is this *Nam?* Is this *Simrin* of Guru Nanak? I am new to myself every time. I remember the Brother. My prayers find their breath from the remembrance of that unselfish service he did me.

No, No. He is the sculptor. I see his song is making and remaking me in the image of Guru Nanak. What can the stone say? What can the clay utter when the Brother is shaping it into beauty? This is the entrance to the Brotherhood the Guru creates. It is in the creation of this Brotherhood and in the entrance into this Brotherhood, that life blossoms up into the universal life of spontaneous, cosmic service. The flower that glows on its stem scents the cosmos. The sun that burns lights up the world. The man that enters into the spirit dissolves himself into the service of the Guru. I see Thee in the wounded. Driven by the irresistible love for Thee, I go and take water to the wounded. Let me nurse the sick, for it is they that lie in bed and groan, so strikingly similar to Thee, O Love. Let me die for joy in Thee, for the love of Thee, for my death shall relieve the whole humanity with a song. I cannot do aught. Of which service can I be to any one? So with the pain of inabilities, I have a tear in my eye, sweet word for all, a kind look, and a sweet running away from all things. Service is my love of Thee. When Thou givest me breath I serve, when Thou withdrawest I fall dead. But no one shall say I had no forgiveness for him, or I was harsh. If a drop of tear can soothe the fire of the rose, I shall weep. If a shower can cool the summer, I will rain down when the Guru bids me. Like a breath of breeze I shall pass on. As air and water and fire and light serve His people, I serve driven by Him. Not of my will, but of His Will shall all service be. The mother serves the child, but the child, too, when he grapples her garment serves the mother. To be happy in the Guru in this unhappy world, to be able to distribute a starry cup of that vital liquid of joy and pain of life, is the highest self-sacrifice and the highest service. 'Naming Him', 'Loving Him' is service. He who is kind is His servant. The Brother soothes the weather-beaten by his touch. He gives a loaf of bread, a smile, a tear and confers thereby an inner sovereignty on the rich and the wretched. He soothes the terrible sorrow of a Hindu widow.

Life begets life. When man sees that rare glimpse of love that the Brother gives, he forgets even his being a leper. He rejoices and rises and prays. The body shall drop. The soul flies on its beautiful wings into the Infinite. A man came who was very learned. He had read books, he had kept vigils, he had gone through the caves of self as the *Yogins* do. He had heard the voice of the caves. And he thought he was big. When he came and saw the Brother who played with children, who talked to young girls and who was abloom like the lotus, drawing the whole Heaven to his heart by a mere look upward, when he saw the pure delight of this spontaneous and easy remembrance, the *Simrin* of the Brother, he knew at a glance that all his life he had been so mean and small. In spite of all his greatness and learning there was to him a revelation of simple truth. He fell at the feet of the Brother. The Brother said nothing to him, just as a mountain says nothing when a pilgrim to the snowy heights kisses the mountain's feet. The glory of all life is in 'the Name'. The whole universe is sustained by 'the Name'. And naming Him with all our senses is love freed from all dross. And love is spontaneous, easy and as cosmic a phenomenon as the formation of suns from the nebulae. In awe of Him, let us be silent. And rapturous like children new-born! To be child-like in trust of Him is the essence of all virtue.

A widow who had just lost her husband came and asked me and you and him, O where is he? Is this wretched separation life? We gave her food, it was gall and wormwood to her. We read stories to her, it made her all the more wretched. We preached to her of Heaven and earth, of God and man, but her distress was unabated. We talked to her like great men of service, of goodness, of being this and that, but her stream of tears flowed on wetting her skirt and sleeves. One 'religion' after another was offered her, she became Hindu, Moslem, Sikh and Christian by turns, but there was no solace. Man again offered her his physical love, but it distressed her all the more. Was her husband not a good enough god of love for her? Was his death not a pain to all human beings as it was to her? Why did they offer her the same physical sorrows of love that the young man of her heart had given her? Did they not feel that the pang he gave her was already infinite? How can one try to soothe it? She was sad philosophically at this heartless spectacle of the so-called religions.

The Brother finds her scratched and bruised and wounded, threadbare, dead. She was utterly disgusted with the worldly wisdom, that its fat and sickening arrogance dominated over the world of religion also in its stupid way. Despairing of God, she was crying to God. The world was full of hunters with their guns levelled against the flying doves. "The cry of the nightingale bereft of her rose was too subtle to be heard". The Brother gave her his love; it was not the love of the young man who had died, it was not the love of the parents who gave her birth, it was not the love of the priest who wanted her to bow down to a particular idol. It was not the love of man, it was the love of the very spirit of the universe. She thought the roses came in crowds to touch her. The stars stretched out their hands to her to bless her and raise her up in a palanquin to the Home of Angels. She saw the running river become kind. The birds looked into her eyes. And though she fled from the society of men, she saw dreams of angels and gods. And sigh after sigh of relief lightened her soul and freed her from the bondage of illusion. She was thenceforward a saint of *Simrin*. She rode a chariot which was taking her through the dawn of a new life unseen before. As the rain-bird has a cry in its throat, she named Him. The widow entered the Brotherhood of Namers. What was it that the Brother had and no one else had? What was it that made the utterance of this word of the Brother different in its vitalising power from the words in the mouths of everyone else and in the books that are on every shelf?

"Find Me and turn thy back on Heaven."

The darkness of sorrow comes like a storm and engulfs me. Nothing avails. I shut my door, light a taper at the alter and sit and watch through the darkness of sorrow the sudden arrival of the Beloved. What they think is fact, reality, is wholly unreal. And what is unreal has in it the symbolic colour of reality. Truly did Vashista say, "O Ramachandra! This sordid real world is the illusion of thy senses. Not for the three times it ever was, is and shall be."

Our very yards and inches with which we measure things and greatness and ethics and life are gone wrong. Let us change our standards.

Mathematics. Two plus two make four. How can such a queer thing be truth? In my mathematics two and two make five or ten or millions!! Such things cannot be anywhere near truth. On the other hand, a beggar maiden of Bikaner with those bead-like black eyes looking wistfully at her lover parting from her, is Truth. It touches some deep chords of my heart and ennobles me, which no books of algebra can ever do. God cannot be a formula. The poor mother surrounded by her children, with tears streaming out of her eyes and the little pearl-like tears out of the children's eyes, these tears and those beads are truth. Their starvation and their tragedy is the mischievous joke of a passing mood of life in its passing shadows. There is the mother radiant, a god. The children are the cherubs of the Garden of Aden. Man is in his blossom. The dew-drops tremble on the fresh-blown roses.

I did not get my body's bread nor had I any clothes but a thread-bare cover of a kind. And I looked askance. The mango tree in blossom smiled at me as no princess beautiful ever looked at her lover from the corners of her eyes. And I laugh and my laughter fills the earth with the gladness of the first dawn.

I am the sacred mansion of the Beautiful. The door to the inner chambers opens to the sacred voice of love. Call me and come in. But if you are of those who wish to desecrate the temple of love, I shut my door and get buried in the glory of my own inner garden of naming Him.

What is the use of repeating His Name? It is a mechanical, tiresome task. To the restless intellect it is just so, perhaps. To the poet, how beautiful is the constant foot-fall of men who go beating a track in the trackless forest, those with soft flesh feet repeating the rhythm of going on and cutting a direction. As the feet of men fall and beat a path, so my lips repeating his name cut a direction for my soul. Sweet is the fall of feet, greater than any music, that beat a path,, but sweeter is the repetition of His name, that by its cadences, cuts a path in regions where no one knows me. This lyrical repetition orientates the axis of life sunward. To the Beloved henceforth, — *in Simrin*. Of what use is building temples to him, if I have not made my body first of all, a temple of His? Every slab here shall have His Name engraven on it. The door of the temple shall be shut to all but those who are of that deep assonance of His Name. They asked me to go and see such and such a man or woman. The Temple has no feet. The Temple stands, and the sun and the moon beat upon its golden cupola. That splendour of the light playing on it, those shivering shades of the *Pipal* and the *Banyan* planted in its courtyard, those sweeps of the woods from the mountains, those beaming faces of the stars. Enough. The temple is under the shade of the presence of the Beautiful ones. I am the aching silence of the Temple. The Brother tells me: "The well is sunk by Him. The lift is put on by Him. The bullocks of that great Gardener work the lift. The fresh water rises and fails and flows. And on the pool I sit and fill the cups and hand them to whosoever comes up thirsty. If any are comforted, I know who is their comforter. The life of the inspiration of service to His devotees is His Mercy to the living who toil in dust like the seeds of flowers to rise in due time and burst into splendid blossoms."

When we part from those we really love, whose sweet remembrance causes deep wounds of life in us, I feel as if *Simrin* of Guru Nanak is like a tender fibre. And where I love, a fibre strikes root in the soil of soul-consciousness. And one small tender fibre in his heart or her heart and one in mine. Centuries pass in separation and after centuries, where there was a little fibre, there stands a huge tree of life. So our feelings are nourished under the deep and mysterious shades of His *Simrin*.

6. SIMRIN, IS THE ONLY BUILDER OF UNSELFISH PERSONALITY

There is another aspect of *Simrin*. The virtuous feel proud and rigid of their well-established and hard-earned virtues. There is a disdain in the movement of their eye-brows as they see those lesser than they in such things. But the man of Guru Nanak's *Simrin* feels how could very Buddhahood be perfect so far as one isolated from the rest of life cannot be perfect? I am the wretched prostitute and I am the cut-throat, I the plunderer, I the meanest, the lowest life struggling upward, Godward. As long as there is one hungry and naked on this earth, how can a true king feel satisfied at the accident of his being well-fed and well-clothed? As long as there is one imperfect, how can a Buddha, the truly awakened, be satisfied in himself with the mere accident of his Buddhahood? The truly great are full of compassion, sympathy, love, never of judgment. When Christ said, "Judge not", it was in the ripe mood of the man of *Simrin* whose omniscience is of the deep unselfish feeling of tender sympathy. This is the mood of *Simrin*. The formalised piety of the Pharisees is the inelastic rigidity of geometrical moral principles which have nothing in common with the cosmic moral law. The professional priests tuck up their sleeves every hour to cast stones at the sinners; they are ugly of soul and blind of heart. Of the cosmic moral law, there is only one thing in us — forgiveness, again forgiveness. Loving alone is the truest service. Naming Him is what is alone beautiful.

Seeing the ocean, we the dwellers on the ponds and the river banks and in the wells get entrance for the winking of an eye into the cosmic consciousness. The little, small geometrical doers of good, who go distributing little cups of water or loaves of bread, get entrance into the mind of the cosmic Giver when suddenly a speck of cloud on the horizon gathers clouds and emits sparks of lightning and floods the whole world. In its furious mercy, it knows no sinner, no saint. Floods pour down. Seeing the man of *Simrin,* the disciples get a glimpse of the cosmic mystery. It opens in the benignant smile of His child-like innocence. The Perfect One is as simple as the speech of a child.

The Hindu worships the cow. But he is unfamiliar with the art of Guru Nanak's *Simrin.* If he knew, he would continuously remember that the cow appropriates just a little dry straw and grass from the universe, and though of such a large body, it is as mild and merciful as a saint. She licks the calf and her hair stands at end with deep spiritual emotion. And she yields. She yields her soul in the form of milk to the calf. To absorb such a sensation of feeling and to emit such spiritual fragrance of motherly love with such a daily pittance of physical needs marks her out as a goddess. If the Hindu knew even the *Simrin* of a cow, he would be as beautiful and as loving as a cow. But he sells her, starves her out to gather dead silver and gold. He is elated when he gets a fortune and depressed when he loses it. His life is not in the divine personality of the cow, but in the dead silver and gold. And then he expects to live amongst the nations of the earth. Dead roots cannot support life. All becomes dry fuel.

The Sikh, too, if he forgets the Guru's art of living, will die like the Hindu. How can one enter the cosmic consciousness without being like an ocean, which sends so much blessing rain and wind to the dwellers on the land? Mark the impetuous altruism of the sea that breaks on the rocks.

The little narcissus has that flower eye. They have not watered the pot. The bulb within the soil is drying, just a little reserve left. The leaves have dried up. The stem too. The little bulb's last resource is exhausted. And the flower still smiles. If we knew the art of *Simrin,* the death of the flower will remind us that no outer circumstances and conditions of life will dim the light of the candle of our heart, which burns the oil of His love of us. The soul within, in blossom of *Simrin* and *Nam* shall only witness our own poverty or opulence, misery or comfort, sorrow or joy, with that supreme indifference with which the human mind can survey the suffering and sorrow or joy of the ages that have gone by and of the people that he has not come into personal and intimate contact with. Even if the soul-blossom, like that of the narcissus, depends on the bulbous reserves of our physical life, it shall use up the last reserve and die like a soldier. Have you not heard Guru Nanak's *Japu?*

> Your age may be long as the four cycles
> And it may be prolonged still ten times more;
> And even if all the nine continents know thy name,
> And even if the people of the whole world follow thee,
> And even if a world-wide reputation and worship await thee in all countries,
> Yet if in the inner regions of the soul thou hast not found the intimacy of His Love, thou art but a worm.

Again:
> Even if thou art as rich as to own a mountain of gold and silver,
> Thou art but a crawling worm compared to one who forgets not Him and who lives in His love, loved by Him.

7. THE ONE THING NEEDFUL

Such in the Guru's mind is the value of all that we so foolishly prize. Are we not then under some self-hypnotism of gross ignorance like the leaping stag dreaming of water in the desert mirage? We are thus bound. When shall we be free? The greatest distress is to be bound by one's own illusions. If the tyrant fetters us and enslaves us, we can scorn the physical suffering he thus inflicts upon us. But how tragic is our self-bondage? I have understood; have you also? When my room is dark, it is the best spiritual act to burn a taper and dispel the gloom, instead of trying to pluck a star from the sky. The woman that sweeps the floors of her house in the morning, lights the evening lamp, and waits by the fireside for the children to be fed, even the father of the children as the eldest son of man for her, is shedding that silence of *Simrin* on the path of life, which abides, which imparts life.

To me, quite uninteresting is the flashy meteoric glimpse of the cinema Star of the modern world. She is called an artist, but as I have said elsewhere, the *Simrin* of Guru Nanak has not yet changed the very measures and standards of men with which they judge their inmost destiny.

Theatre and drama and cinema are not those arts which impart life. They spend it. They make of the human personality a mere firework. They are the acts and literatures of the poor geometrical minds of men. Only the empire-building nations like the Romans and the British produce such poor literatures. There is and can be no lyrical racial genius in such people, whose consciousness goes gathering only the wool of illusions. They are as a race incapable of any high life-giving bible-like divine lyrical literature. It is by fortunate snatches of the higher life that we are unawares put in touch with the cosmic mind. Literature and art that are created by minds not filled with the cosmic sympathy or information are only of ephemeral, intellectual interest which grows dim or intense according to our capacity for spending on them our life-substances of that inner richness of soul.

Every people have their literature of geometrical consciousness for the excitement of intellectual interests and pleasures. And also they have the literature of the cosmic consciousness, which, however less bright, less coherent, less complex, less clever in expression, is life-giving. The New Testament, especially the reputed words of Christ, have in them that wonderful quality which no other writer in the west, poet or prose-writer, has. I repeat what I have said in my *The spirit of Oriental Poetry*[1], that but for the words of the Bible, the people of the west would have died of starvation of the soul. The noble mother reading the Bible by the bed of her sick child, lifting up her eyes bedewed with team, is the living symbol of Mary. This consolation amidst death and despair, misery and distress of life is not to be found in Shakespeare, or in Swinburne, nor in Keats nor Shelley. They all must bend their knees and kiss the feet of Christ. They must pour ointment at His feet and rub them with their hair if they are men. The literature they create is like the babble of children. I may be wild and mad, but none of these geniuses has that quality which I cannot name, but can only suggest.

With us, the Sikhs, *Guru Grantha* is that book to which there is no equal from the oldest *Vedas* to the latest books. For, no one in India ever has been so cosmic in the quality of his mind as Guru Nanak. He is the whole moral nature incarnate. He is not a speech nor a song, but a moral cosmos. He is the whole spirit. The infinite contradiction in His thoughts on men and things crossing their lines and even the planes of thought coming and cutting each other at an infinite number of little points, now holding out the law of *Karma,* then dashing It down like a fragile snow-ball, now saying this is truth and then saying this is not truth, moments crossing the days, the days the years, years eternity, one sweet mood contradicted by another still more fresh and still more new — gives to the thought and composition of *Guru Grantha* the cosmic colour which baffles all attempts at analysis of its understanding by analysis. Beyond language, beyond meaning, its whole design goes and fascinates the soul by an endless repetition and taking hold of man from within, makes of him a God.

So far I have been a victim of the intellectual and merely analytical doubt of the modern do-nothings, the argue-about-and-about table-talkers, that the repetition of the Guru's words is at times but mechanical and I still hold that the dead uninspired priest and theologian do still make it so. But when the personal love of the Guru inspires you, repetition is the only provision for the lonely traveller of life. And all are lonely. The word of Guru Nanak is the companion of eternity. The more we live with it, the richer we grow. We go about repeating our actions and daily thoughts, and the repetition yields ever fresh pleasures of life. And so if we first become alive with the spark of His love, all our repetition is like the repetition of our acts and thoughts of love. Repetition gives new clothes to our feeling. And the singing of His Psalms is like travelling on a path, going onward to Him.

They who are incessant readers of His Book are of the rare class of the great saviours of men. All others, in spite of their intellectual brilliance and cleverness, are of the common class of sufferers. I have, by the grace of the Guru, found in this life, at last at the age of 48 years, that for the Sikh, beginning to love Him is the first day of the new spiritual birth. And repetition of His Word and Name, not losing a single breath, a single step, is the life spiritual growing through mud and dust upward, springing up like the lotus in the infinite sunshine and air above. Above there! As the new born baby learns the language of the mother, so has the disciple to learn of this spirit and inspiration of the Guru and in this effortless effort is the secret of living in deep musical unison with the Guru. When I was a child, I lisped incoherently, incorrectly, His Name. When now an adult, I wish to repeat His name ceaselessly. The intellectual student of spirituality may call it useless. I fain would run away from him and buried in my comparative ignorance repeat the name of the Beloved.

I would also run away from the theologian and that quaint species of man in Eastern countries who sit in caves and meditate on *nothing* without their limbs and bodies becoming fluid like the river water, flowing with His song in living tearful sympathy and tenderness of love, who have not seen the union of love! The *modus operandi* is the repetition of His Name, *Simrin, or Aching Remembrance.* "Without Him, my soul takes fire and is reduced to ashes," says Guru Nanak. "The tongue that is not lyrical in repetition of His Name, had better be cut into ribbons," says Guru Arjan Dev. And yet they say, "Without feeling, how can one attain to perfection?" Guru Gobind Singh says, "You, You. *Tuhi! Tuhi!*" As the new bride desires her young bridegroom, with that passionate passiveness the man of *Simrin* is to wait for Him. Waiting is *Simrin.* And quivering passionate waiting! But is that passiveness?

The wedded woman is not restless, for she has attained to the spontaneous perfection of wedded life. Her act of loving her husband is continuous. There is no theatricality, no show to mar her remembrance of him. So, says Guru Nanak, is the spontaneous lyrical life of a disciple of *Simrin.*

Even by wedding with her husband, the wedded woman essentially lives by remembrance of Him — *Simrin.* For, separate bodies separate them, as space separates. So, even, nestling close to him, she is only remembering Him. What we call loving each other is only in intense moments but acts of *Simrin.*

This world is a museum in which I, the man, have found the complete fulfilment of all my desires. What folly it is for me to desire to be king when one of my own self, a man with a similar constitution, is there already a king! And when I see that by no means doth a mere kingdom add a cubit to the stature of man! I desire renunciation of all this and to be a poor man. I have only to turn my eyes and look at thousands like me passing through that fulfilment. Mere wretchedness of poverty and squalor adds nothing to man nor subtracts aught from him.

If I study myself and all these myriad postures of achievement and unfulfilment of my aims and desires, I cannot but shudder at the disaster of the soul laid bare before me by my desires and struggles at achievement! I desire nothing. I am well where I am. Only, I will burn myself like the temple lamp. As the rose flames on its own mother twig, I only flame up and live in the glow of life. *Simrin* is thus a spiritual attitude. As the dog has an upward tendency to love man, so the man of *Simrin* has an upward tendency to the gods above him. The maintenance of an activity to respond to the touches of love, to the calls of love, to the tender soft compassionate look of love, from the Higher ones is as the bride's preparation to meet the bridegroom. His Name is repeated by my eyes that look for His coming and my very flesh blossoms in the repetition of His Name, who is coming, coming!

The intense affirmation of Prahlad by his noble, undaunted repetition of His Name points to the perpetual spring that rolls in the soul of the man of *Simrin* and all his being is deluged with joy whose sorrow of love is infinite.

Guru Gobind Singh says that the sustenance divine of *Nam* which enabled the courtesan Ganika to swim across the sea of darkness, that the very naming Him is his support of life. So the man of *Simrin* — the Guru's disciple, lays no claim to any exaltation of soul, which, by a similar opening out of one's self to the infinite glory of the Beloved, cannot be shared equally by the flower, the bird. He judges not. A miserable prostitute has the inalienable right to name Him and be comforted as has the saint. It is possible her spirit by absolute indifference to the life of the body may provide wings in an unexpected manner to soar above the sordid conditions of life, If we view things critically, are not all of us more or less helpless as a common prostitute and as miserable? It is not in the churches, nor in the temples but in man's own shrine of the heart within, where he, having cast off all outer clothes of piety and impiety, of evil and of good, enters into the pure nudity of soul, and sees face to face His personal God, his Guru.

There is a lotus abloom in the shrine of the heart. To the man of *Simrin*, his eyes, like live bees hover within. A million flowers may call them away, but they cannot rise out of there. They cannot fly; satiated, drunk and drinking the light of the lotus, they are dead yet alive. *Simrin* is, thus, living inward, with Open eyes, yet seeing naught of the outside. Have you seen the eyes of Beethhoven? It is a rare spiritual intensity. This love transmutes all sorrows into flames of life. The realization of suffering and the solace of *Nam* to cool down the fires of misery are of the divine treasures. The man of *Simrin* is deeply altruistic for by *Simrin* he has gathered the substance of life, which comforts the heavy-laden and the weary. Guru Arjan Dev says in *Sukhmani*, "*Nam* is the only form that compassion can take, for *Nam* gives the power to lessen human misery."

Standing on the seashore, I saw how the waves that rise are of some immense joy and how they break endlessly. With all the waves of the mind rising and melting down in me, if I carry them like flowers of foam and place them at His feet, and break like the sea, I am of *Simrin*. In *Simrin* therefore it is the immensity of mind flowing in one direction, that matters. I do not run after making my sea of self calm or disturbed, these two things depend on controls other than my own, but I take care that I like the sea to break at His feet like melted wreathes of foam of joy and be not myself.

They think of many things all the hours of physical living, who do not repeat His Nam physically by the tongue. They repeat wandering thoughts. And the choice lies between thinking naught and thinking many things. The Guru has as the symbol of the mind, the white hawk. The white hawk is let free when it has to go after the prey, but it perches on His thumb when it has not to fly after the prey. So the mind like the engine of a car must work full swing onward.

But it must be immediately declutched, the moment its activity is not required. The clothes of many thoughts must be put off and the unclothed soul dipped in the sunshine and the moonshine and the liquid blue of the Infinite. Why put the sand and rubbish of unnecessary and unproductive worry into the cog-wheels of the mind and be so uneasy about life? Learn to declutch your mind and soul from the burdens you have to carry. And that can be through *Simrin*. It is by the continuous vibration of feelings that man is made whole, holy.

People wish to hear of beautiful things, but they do not generally relish the simple processes of the *modus operandi* of realizing such delectable states of life. But all the same in spite of high intellectual flights, the acutest and the subtlest of intellects have to play like monkeys in matters of the deepest concern in life, before which intellectual pursuits look like shoes that are not allowed within the sanctuary. The pleasures of repeating our facial acquaintances with those who are ours or of whom we are in any measure, come to us by repetition so simply that we are hardly conscious how much life comes to us through our pleasures. How many times have we seen the scenery of the hill and the lake, of the human face, and how many times more still do we not desire their repetition? By repetition, suddenly, a new standard of beauty flashes upon us and we thank someone for being alive to have been lucky enough to see such a new miracle of a shining face or a bright aspect of the divine face. Life crystallizes into delightful shapes of beauty by *Simrin*. And there are grades. The creeper clinging to a tree, the wife to the arm of her husband, the child to the finger of his mother, are all the tendencies of *Simrin*. And so are the monuments raised to the heroes and so are the temples raised to God, and songs sung in praise of great and glorious acts of man.

"No one is truly mine," says Guru Teg Bahadur. Let me cling to Him and Him to me. There is inner, companionship of soul unconditional, subjective and everlasting.

Perishable is all that you, O man, venture out of your soul to own. And without *Simrin*, let me tell you, you cannot truly own yourself. Then up and gather the nuts of life, these hard things of repeating His Name and after death, you will know what great treasures you have gathered in the nuts of *Nam*. And those who have gathered other things, will find their empty hands besmeared with soot. The quality of the soul shall determine your position in the universe, not your possessions, however beautiful. I have seen it. I ran away from this tedious task of repetition. But without it, without this symbolic act of love, I had no more passage into the Garden where He dwells. So I was thrown down the mountain, into the fire for all my elevated talk. And through suffering at the hands of my love I have learnt that His *Nam* and its repetition is the root and all else the branches, leaves and blossoms. Without having a living root I am a fibre cut off and put in a vase and my brilliance of any kind is but dying. *Simrin* is engrafting ourselves on the roots of life; and then endeavour not. It grows in spite of ourselves. It blossoms in spite of ourselves.

Thus, one thing is needful, all else is added unto us.

Footnotes:

1. *The Spirit of Oriental Poetry*, Punjabi University, Patiala, 1969.

IV

'ASA-DI-VAR' OF GURU NANAK

In this theme of the eternal what is miscalled 'religion' from time immemorial is cast aside. The sacred thread folly is mercilessly exposed. The hypocritical readings of scriptures and the wearing of loose garments and the painting of foreheads and the reservation of cooking squares, the wrong emphasis on dietary and human secretions, the theatricalities of devotion, are thrown away forever as unworthy of any serious notice as religion or as religious. The old impertinent rocks of all such ignorance are shattered by the Guru's bolt and made to form the bed of His river of peace to flow through. This is *Asa-di-Var*—the freedom of mind attained by imbibing the glory of truth, new with every new sunrise.

It is for us to drink with both our palms cupped up, the peace of the Dawn that breaks for us in the hymns of *Asa-di-Var*.

You remember how Bhai Nand Lal saw the face of Guru Gobind Singh and then could not find anything more beautiful. In His presence, for Bhai Nand Lal, the sun, that great orb that lights the physical universe, was dark. It was all dark without the Guru.

Once when the Guru was organizing the militia of his saint-soldiers of the Punjab, Bhai Nand Lal came and placed before the Guru a sword and a belt and begged that he too may be enlisted as the Guru's soldier in the Guru's armies of saints. It was a pathetic scene when the Guru went in with the sword and the belt and returned to Bhai Nand Lal with a pen, saying, "Nand Lal, you take this pen, I will wear your sword for you." And with this golden pen the poet got from Him, he wrote songs of the Ineffable Beauty. He, so to say, sang out his soul in shining streams of that liquid fire of love.

Asa-di-Var sings of such sensitive soul, such personal love of the great.

Asa-di-Var kindles, like the sun, the gloom of centuries. The Guru has given us great lyrics, to sing them with full throat in the wild tunes of our Majha and Malwa prairies, which is our greatest privilege of life. To let their holy sound dissolve in our blood and in the blood of our children and our children's children is simple and spontaneous gratitude to Him, the Giver. We were in the darkness, the *Guru* lighted our homes with lamps of joy. The Guru made us *Vihangams*, eagles; he gave us wings. The Guru truly freed us in His love of us.

If we live now without the great majestic spirit of freedom, He gave us, we are wretched with all our wealth and our political doctrines. The Guru told us, better death than a life of slavery, better death than a life of compromise with Satan. They gave up their lives and the lives of their children and their disciples and even the truth they came to free man with and for which the greatest of men make compromises with the world to spread it amongst the people, even that personal truth they shattered into a million atoms like a ball of snow, of a strange divine efflorescence, only to tell you that the freedom of the human soul was above all things. All must go, and the human soul must find its freedom.

God's message can well go back to Heaven and return, but there shall be no compromise with falsehood on matters of the absolute freedom of the human soul.

In this song-gift, the Guru has poured out the great power that brings freedom. Slaves sang it, they became free. We can sing it now and be free. If we are not free yet, we have hot yet known this song. Perhaps a too theological atmosphere put round the Guru's hymns, perhaps a too Brahmanical ecclesiastical interpretation given to the hymns of freedom, all such things of inertia and old habits, have tended to deaden us to the infinite freshness of *Asa-di-Var*.

True feeling is infectious. How does a new born Japanese child get the fervour of a whole nation for his national anthem? The fervour is imparted to every embryo in every mother's womb; it is there that men are made or marred. To be indifferent for an hour, as a Sikh, is to make generations of Sikhs indifferent. How great is our responsibility to burn the lamp of the Guru, day and night, within the temple of our heart. If the Sikh Brotherhood were still inspired, no young Sikh boy could be indifferent to the rhythm of his soul. The young minds complain of a dead theological routine, but they don't tell us, how else they would become more fervent for the ideals of the Guru. Replace the theological dead routine by some enthusiasm of the rising youth. Young men! if the present generation of men has gone wrong, you go right. But pray go right. Have you ever suspected that your cry against this discipline of love imposed upon you by your seniors may be a cry of license for indolence? If the present generation of men have not grasped the significance of the hymns of the Guru, you should rise all the more with deadly resolve to vindicate your spiritual ancestry.

You be what they have not been. Love is always spontaneous. And you can judge yourself how genuine love finds its way to the Beloved. Spring, as a poet says, is His letter. How much more His Hymns! The other day, a young Sikh asked me, "Of what use is repeating *Japu*?" I had a copy of *Japu* with me. I pressed it to my bosom in a frenzy and I replied, "If we can sleep on it as John slept on the knee of Jesus, certainly do not repeat it. But if you love the Guru, what is the way to reach Him? Lie at His feet, and like a babe cry out His hymns,—is this not the symptom of love? If you do not feel like it, you are simply defending your want of passion, and passionate loyalty to the person of your Liberator!"

Now to the *Asa-di-Var*. The Guru transmutes his Sikh, makes a man into an angel. This transmutation of the metal of man is at the basis of this great inspiration to which nominally and possibly merely out of social convention we now belong. Truly, only the inspired ones belong to it, whatever their name or colour or creed. No spiritual outlook comes to the blinded man till in the firmament of his soul rises the Guru-Sun and dispels the gloom. All is dark without Him. It is just like Dante's picture of Paradise, without Beatrice all is dark. If Beatrice is not seen by him in the shining comets, he finds his soul is being destroyed. Heaven shines if she shines. This is the secret of *Dhyanam* of Him. When you do not feel you are in glowing passion for Him, know that you are going away from God to Satan. Your soul-consciousness is being petrified like Ahalya of the *Ramayana*, or like that of the heroine of *Gul-i-Bakaoli*.

The curse is upon you and you are becoming stolid, sordid, stone-dead. The beautiful love-mood is gone and you, be as clever as you like, the Guru says, you are like the empty sesame that are left in the fields unharvested. Their core is fungus-eaten and all their inside is rust, black rust.

Creation is viewed by Guru Nanak as His handicraft. There is the divine, beautiful, cosmic spirit of the universe, the soul, that creates out of *itself* investing all His creation with the mystery of that Great Oneness of self, mystery of Beauty, out of which is born Love which *personalises* the cosmic spirit of the universe. He creates love by his glances on his own handicraft.

Guru Nanak then says, "This *here* is truth. Whatever thou seest is He, is Truth. Forms are real. The continents are real. The swinging cosmos is Truth. His court is of Truth, His law is Truth."

All this and all that, the naked things are wondrous. All things are made of wonder, they excite wonder.

"The sky arches," says Guru Nanak, "in awe of Him, the law, the Truth." He alone is above all laws. It is by His favour that one meets the Guru. The Guru awakens the universal life in us and one realises Truth, one foregoes self and 'the *Universe grows* I.' And this realization comes by meeting the Guru.

Again and again the Guru says, without the Guru no one gets to the life. By the favour of the Guru I drop the vanity of self and its local self-hypnotisations. Meeting the Guru has extinguished the life of separation. By him man finds the soul of the universe. This one thing is needful. Without it all scholarship is vain, in vain the reading of cartloads of books. Education is but sickness, pilgrimage is a weariness of the flesh. Fasting is an unnecessary privation of the flesh. In pious vows of silence man sinks down into morbid stupors and how can, the Guru 'says, without the Guru, one's soul wake up to the essential virtues? Without that awakening the blinded man, says the Guru, loses his soul for nothing. When he meets the Guru, he gets the spiritual attitude which is peace.

Without the spirit of truth burning in the heart of man, all is a lie. The king, the country, the law, the people, all are lies. These bodies, the striving raiments of youth will be left on this shore;'\ we have to go to the shore yonder. One has ruled over others as he listed, but the path beyond is. narrow and when he is face to face with his own self there, he repents having done so many acts against the purity of his own soul. Then the Guru announces that forgiveness is the great act of the true spiritual attitude. His sacred thread with which man is to be twice-born, reborn of spirit, is made of Daya—forgiveness. Guru Nanak's ethics are founded on the effects of men and things on one's own self-consciousness. Hatred wounds the soul. All evil causes deep fissures which take centuries to heal. For one's own sake, one has to be good at the bayonet's point. Though not to-day, to-morrow he must. Purity is the natural state of being, like the crystal stream just born in the mountains. And it is not they that wash clean or dress clean but the pure of the spirit that are truly pure. Slander no one, never indulge in reducing others in your own eyes. Only understand and pass on.

And the mineral kind of purity as of the diamond and the sun to which the Yogis and the Brahmans aspire is lifeless compared with the Guru's love and the living impulse of the spirit of comradeship the Guru planted thick in his goodness. They, the Brahmanical ascetics, had denounced woman to transcend sex. The Guru transcends sex through sex. Woman, says the Guru, is the centre of life here on earth and in Heaven. Man is born of woman, He is wedded to woman. How can woman go out of the spiritual court, who gives birth to all the spiritual geniuses of the world? All are so constituted in sex. Only that Great Unborn Cosmic Spirit is above sex. Talking slander as they do of woman is to slander one's soul. They who speak ill make only themselves ill. The dirt that sticks to one's soul is not washed by bathing in a thousand sacred rivers. The good ones do not emphasize the outer wear. If the soul is rich, the body may be howsoever poor, what reck they?

What is that *gift* which we earn by our own efforts. Accomplishments cannot be in the nature of spiritual gifts, they are achievements. What is truly miraculous is the gathering of those harvests which we have never sown. All others take refuge in their own *Karma* and are proud of what they become thereby, good or bad. The Guru imparts faith. There is a higher universe with which we are knitted. And not by our own *Karma*, but by His *Karma*. The miraculous is to strike friendship with the Higher Ones of Heaven, not with ourselves. The miraculous is to get love from them. Loving, according to the Guru, is only the unfulfilled half, the fulfilled whole is *being loved.*

The Guru's sayings cannot be exhausted by any amount of interpretations. A million new and varied interpretations leave them as fresh as ever. They are truly creations of art and any one of us can look at them and have his heart-cup full of meaning and direction and love and miracle and whatever he may desire.

And by saying what I have said in this way of *Asa-di-Var,* I have only indicated the wealth we have, and we know not.

V

THE MESSAGE OF 'SUKHMANI' OF GURU ARJUN DEV

Guru Arjun Dev has sent us a Hymn of peace. It is like a river of peace in which we can dip our soul. Bathing is a mechanical process, sometimes we do no feel like bathing. But whenever we bathe, we feel refreshed. We feel new. We love ourselves. The clogged pores of the body are cleaned. The mind, too, becomes rectified by a mechanical process. I feel when we read *Sukhmani,* there is, unknown to ourselves, a strange effect on our minds. And there is a reflex action on the body. The mind mounts up to some delectable heights and the body becomes light and ethereal and soars with it. We feel bodiless. In this river of peace, we must plunge daily and refresh ourselves. And when the mind is risen, we should kiss in every line and in every word the beautiful hands of our King who composed it for us. No hymns can give one the love-spark unless they belong to oneself. The French national song belongs to every French child and man and woman. When they all stand and sing, they become inspired thereby. So is the case with the Japanese national anthem. Songs fly away like birds without love's fond ownership. Especially so is the case with this most sensitive song—*Guru Grantha*. He will not live with the dead as a mere book. Now we must in a similar way, feel an intense personal love for this great universal anthem of Guru Arjun Dev. The Guru does not sing of a nation here, nor of kingdoms, nor of war cries or of the victory yells of conquerors. It is a hymn which is to set all the loose screws of humanity right. Once, I was very much upset about a business that I was running. The people who worked with me were idiots. The neighbours vexed me. The friends taunted me, cursed me. The contractors cheated me. The financiers failed me, they always fail when it does not pay them to help others. Friends were either poor or indifferent. I had for days become as one insane. I fell out with everybody on the slightest provocation. I lost my temper on every little mishap. My nerves were over-strung. I had no sleep for many nights. I thought I was going mad. My servants thought that such unhingement would drive me to a lunatic asylum. They were all anxious about my mental health. Such was my condition. The clouds came, the cold wind from the North came. I laughed. My eyes closed. I took up the hymn of *Sukhmani* and began reading it. I went on and gave its own lilt to my soul. It lent a sweetness to my voice. My face that was over-cast with the dark stains of sins of unattunement began glowing. All *stains* were burnt up. I felt light and gay again like a bird. And I thought that the singing of *Sukhmani* was a great cure for human failing out. That insane mind into which business worries had driven me comes upon nations, they lose temper and they go to war and kill millions. Before they lose all control, if they could bathe in lyrical river of Guru Arjun Dev, the world could be set right. For a member of an enslaved nation to say this might sound presumptuous, but I am speaking of the hymns of the King. Even a slave can have the joy in him to chant the praise of the King. Even a slave can set fire if he has a torch burning in his eyes. We cannot take out the Golden Temple everywhere. There is exquisite peace when the moon comes and lies on the golden dome and sees her face in the blue lake around. There is peace when the sun conceals itself within the temple and makes its very walls burst with a strange radiation that is caught by the little waves around. If the modern riff-raff of the human element were absent, the Golden Temple is an ideal pictured in marble. It is a Presence. The spiritual effects of that silent presence are marvellous and only those who are in tune with the Hymn of the Master, know how the broken threads of the lyrical silence of the soul are set right by a mere touch. Pilgrims send in their smoke and dirt and breath. The Temple, like a flowing river, washes all that away. It is a perennial holiness. Guru Ram Das built it, Guru Arjun Dev completed it. And he made it the home of His songs. He sang them here with His *tambura*. Here the heavenly beings came to listen to the songster. Here they still come. The spiritual effects are due to the constant visits of the holy beings, the liberated ones. Such is the dream of the Golden Temple, *Hari-Mandir!*

But the whole of it stands in sound in *Sukhmani*. *Sukhmani* is the *Hari-Mandir* built in song. It has the spiritual atmosphere of the presence of the celestials. And those who read *Sukhmani* to meet those angels meet them in its music. I don't say that the daily reading of it like the *Namaz* of the old *Kazi* of Sultanpur, is any graceful act. Gratitude demands that we should live, move and have our being in its rhythm. *If we are sweetened by the Ideal, daily reading is power, occasional reading is love and not reading it at all is Union.* Not reading is the most difficult. Occasional reading is getting into a rage of love. And daily reading is husbanding the powers which may be required by the Master whenever He may so will. But, surely, reading like the *Namaz* of that old *Kazi* even five times a day is making, to take a lesser example, '*La Marsellaise*' of the French dead by repeating it without the required pitch of the music of a nation's soul behind it or with it. It is the occasion that lends its power to music. *Sukhmani* has to be sung by us with a communal glow of our soul as His disciple. We have to make ever new beautiful approaches to the Hymn. May I here tell you how the artistic people of Japan honour songs. The brief poetic flights of *Uta* composers are honoured in a unique way. One song on 'The moon' composed by a tea-master was to be so welcomed. The tea-master invited a few friends—friends who were also attuned to that unknown harmony, not the usual curious 'bores', they were song-strung friends, inebriate with lyrical culture. And it was midnight. They sat on the simple straw-mats of Japan in a spiritual room, free from the vexation of furniture. And a beautiful picture of the moon with that *Uta* song written on it, a-hanging on the wall was already there, but no one saw it. It was to be a revelation of beauty. When? None of the guests knew. Suddenly the host slided the *shop*, the sliding door of the room, and the moon in the sky came~~ down as a poem in the room. All admired the *Uta*. It gave them all an ecstasy of silent appreciation. You can well see when an *Uta* needs so much welcome, how much more must be your artistic accomplishment to welcome the song of *Sukhmani*. On the other hand, you are wholly unprepared for it. Thanks to the vow of some good men who read it daily, there is the sense of some ownership still with you. But it is like the owning by a boor of a huge beautiful diamond which he uses to weigh vegetables with.

Like *Guru Grantha*, whose one hymn has the same sculptured idea in it, as is inlaid in the whole of *Gum Grantha*, *Sukhmani* too is the repetition of beautiful songs of the same. One sun of the face of the Beloved. But the very first message, both of *Guru Grantha* and *Sukhmani*, is not the *meaning* but the music of the beautiful. As when a beautiful woman suddenly appears before you, it is the music of her personality which thrills you, not the meaning. Music is higher than poetry in this sense. Poetry has meaning, but the highest poetry or music has no meaning, it has a subjective presence of the beautiful. It is the setting of a right spiritual attitude in us. It is the music of the Beautiful, the peace that the meeting with the Beloved gives. If a lost son comes home, and the mother goes up and meets him, there is an atmosphere of ecstasy suddenly precipitated. That tearful thankful ecstasy of the meeting is the kind of musical approach we have to make to *Sukhmani*. I am not telling of physical things. When Laila comes and meets Majnu, it gives Majnu a madness of joy in which he forgets himself. The intense love which abstracts us from ourselves is the requisite sweetness for reading the music of *Sukhmani*, A thirsty longing to meet Guru Arjun Dev, a dumb wish to go barefooted to see Him, are preparations for the song of *Sukhmani* It is music and it requires music in us to dare approach it. And I tell you of the music of union which is the highest, intensest passion of the human soul.

Musical attunement with our environment, musical inebriation, and a lyrical life of love, —these are the effects of the ownership of *Sukhmani*. He who owns a kingdom of the soul has the joy of it. There is a pride that *La Marseillaise* and the Japanese national anthem pour into the blood of the people. So he or they who own *Sukhmani* do not become Indian or Japanese or English, but men with the music of soul ringing in them. Wherever they are, there can be no discord, no noise. A lyrical atmosphere envelops their lives, they will die if that sweet peace, that moonlight beauty, departs. They live in the music of love. Political rights bang out of doors. All rights are wrong if my soul loses its lustre. If the atmosphere of *Sukhmani* departs from my temple of flesh, the world is a grave-yard for me. This great jealousy of the artist for inspiration belongs to every owner of *Sukhmani*. When the inebriation of my song is gone out of me, when the joy of my art is lost, of what use is life? Better a lead bullet in my heart than a day, an hour, a moment without the Beloved.

So we are called upon by *Sukhmani* to preserve ourselves, to maintain that temple-atmosphere within us.

Tell me, what is the meaning of the river in flow, of a song in its flight? Is it not foolish for us to seek the meaning of the sky and the stars, when their mere sight is music for the soul? *Sukhmani*, I tell you, is something of the same beautiful kind. To see beauty is to know it. To love beauty is to be beautiful. The beautiful is the whole truth. When it is put in a particular dialect, how is this music to become universal? Just as Nature, in spite of a thousand and a hundred thousand languages, makes the music of life universal. The beautiful woman requires no particular speech to be loved everywhere. But with this difference. The song of Guru Arjun Dev is to be embodied by us, and for us. And it is the sight of the reader of *Sukhmani* that shall make the music of *Sukhmani* universal for man. By seeing the son, they shall see the father. If you cannot produce the type of man which *Sukhmani* or for the matter of that *Guru Grantha* invokes, you will die and the song shall die also because in its dialect it is so local. The translation of such things is through men living the great love-inspired life. The Bible and its translations are meaningless, it is the lyrical life of faith that the Christian saints lived which created that great cathedral in Europe, the Bible. Man is to be saved by man, no gods shall ever come to help him. Unless men are cast in the divine lyrics, unless there is an artistic chiselling of the shapeless marble, there can be no lyrical activity in society. Without lyrical activity *Sukhmani* cannot live with you long. The white swan of *Mansarovar* shall fly away from you, if you open not your breast and show him the *Mansarovar* of your heart. Mechanical repetition is stupid unless supported by the lyrical activity of the inner active silence of shaping ourselves in the image of our father. The measure of man's worth is this development of his artistic consciousness and its creativeness. And the highest art is to be beautiful, not so much to draw good pictures or make fine images. And *Sukhmani* is the music that creates the beautiful in us. Unless everyone is more than Joseph, unless the whole world thirsts for a glimpse of your Zuleikha, of what use is being called 'Sikhs', who have that glorious hymn, the one large hymn of the Gurus, *Gum Grantha*. The Greeks created beautiful images and they dominate the whole of the European civilisation of Art; its ideals are all Hellenic. Hellenism is the religion of Europe. The Greek did not hunt after empires like Rome. Rome dug its own grave, but Greece with her sense of beauty has carved out an empire in the eternity of human feeling.

O young Sikhs I remember what they of the common run seek is nothing worth seeking. They sought all such things and perished. Those who seek Him are worthy of respect. This is the message of *Sukhmani*, but how many of us hear it? The Master Himself anticipates, only one in millions. But young men, you may be that, one in millions. Millions of you must seek it and one shall find it and thus the search of millions shall bear a rare fruit. This is the meaning when the Guru says, "rare is the genius of true art."

VI

READINGS FROM 'SUKHMANI'—
THE CHARMED GEM OF PEACE

Love is, according to the Guru, an ineffable glow of the soul, wholly subjective in its nature and self-contained and is the final fulfilment of life, which, in itself is capable of infinite refinement and infinite responsiveness. It is the seed-God sprouting in man, from which axial point it develops vertically into an infinite mystery. All else of man, of earth, is engulfed by this growth of Grace. Man dies. God wakes up. The human body is the temple thenceforward, and all acts of man are acts of pure worship. If he eats, it is in continuous music of a shining dedication; if he breathes, it is utter thankfulness in a fatal kind of sweetness stealing over him. He cannot be but full of ambrosia. He is the lover. An infinite pang makes all this earth holy. And, the Guru says this love is inspiration. It comes like the light, it flows like a stream from the unknown depths. It is not obtained through any power nor through any accomplishment; it is not the result of *Karma;* it is the Grace of God, the Guru. And in this sense of the Guru being the fountain head, the disciple has to look up to him. He is the Beloved. This infinite looking up to Him is what the Guru calls *Simrin* or remembrance of Him. And the Guru says that the remembrance of Him, the 'Naming of Him', is love, and that there is no other form of love so pure on this earth.

The *loves* we know of are mere symbols of this great peace of Self-realization. They are some far off glimpses. Pure youth dedicated to loving is so near to this glow of soul that one is tempted to identify the youth's passion with it. The Guru's hymns are redolent with these symbols of human passion. The Bride and the Bridegroom are two words in which this spiritual glow of Guru Nanak finds a cheerful expression. There is nothing else in which his infinite pang can transmute itself into an abiding, unfading joy of life. We do remember even subconsciously our beloved ones lost to our sight, even in utter forgetfulness of the daily rush, and we remember them in proportion as we love them. Moments are not wanting, even for us mortals, when an intensity compels us to faint away in that remembrance, in an involuntary renunciation of all other pursuits. And we live by remembrance then. In that remembrance, as Emerson says, we build a new universe with our passion, we feel the blood of the rose flowing in our veins and a kind of infinite sympathy overpowers our whole system. This poor remembrance is also a symbol of that *Simrin* of which Guru Nanak tells us and in which intensity he swings the star-lit cosmos as a garland of lamps in worship of His Beautiful Beloved. Similarly, you will see, we sweeten our days in this rocky wilderness of human life on this earth, with a few names of our friends that are dear to us. The names, as realities of our consciousness and not as syllables of any language, are dear truths. Deprive us of one of our beloved ones and how sorrowful does our life become? And, this sorrow too is a symbol of the great pang of Guru Nanak, who says, "Forgetting His Name, I get wholly burnt up."

These symbols of our love and our human relationships just enable us to imagine what the Guru's great inspiration of love is like. It is imagination through which we can reach the soul. Reaching our soul, we reach the soul of the universe. And *Sukhmani* is our high white mountain where God, our Guru, dwells and in its chant we reach the Unreachable.

The anthem flows in an ambrosial stream of hope and light from the bosom of Guru Arjun Dev. The glory of the day-break is a symbol of the great illumination that, like a holy nimbus surrounds this hymn of the Guru.

When one gets that inspiration from on high, a little grain, a shining grain comes and impregnates the soul; it is the seed of the eternal, it is the shining nucleus of Godhead. The life of the disciple takes its start. Beyond all description is the state of such an inspired Being. Peace is remembrance of Him. Health of body and mind is remembrance of Him. Love is the cure of all ills. This peace, this love is found nowhere, but in the heart.

Washed away by this streaming glory and its infinite sweetness is the disease of human smallness. Rent asunder are the fetters of the human ego that creates its own bondage. Freedom from death and decay comes to the soul of man. Man wakes up to love's infinite responsiveness. One rises above all fear, and above all sorrow and suffering.

And this remembrance of Him comes truly to him who is in full assonance with the saint who lives this life. And the music of this spiritual harmony is the all-providing treasure of God.

Such remembrance of Him is spiritual accomplishment. And in it are resumed *Gyan* and *Dhyan*. The intellect mounts high and is sharpened by the illumination coming from behind, through an all-awakened intuition.

This is worship, this is religion, this is all. In the remembrance, the duality of human consciousness is lost and one bathes truly in a sea of joy. In the higher spiritual world, he is honoured who lives attuned to this music of life. Whatever such any one does, is musical, Is good. Life bears all its fruits in this state of infinite Naming Him.

But only they are inspired of remembrance of Him, whom He so favours;
It is His divine dispensation!

Desire dies. Knowledge is spontaneous there. The heaviness of soul is washed away there and the mind becomes pure, when His Name shines within. That Lord of Love, that Beloved lives in the voice of the saints. His throne is the tongue of the saints of *Simrin*. They have the true wealth who have Him. They are truly men of honour. Heaven accepts them who accept His love. They are rich and need nothing of this world.

They are the kings of this universe,
And they have entered this path of remembrance, whom He hath so admitted.
Those who thus live, move, and have their being in love, in remembrance of Him, are the salt of this earth, they are the true servants of humanity.
They have searched many scriptures and law books,
But nothing approaches in spiritual value anywhere near it, this great love of Him.
A whole *Ashtpadi* is devoted as an ode to the saint of *Simrin*.

"In his presence," says the Guru, "the face beams up, the soul shines of itself. All dust and dirt of *Karma* is washed away. God, the Guru, comes close to man and nestle close to Him. One feels a spontaneous fascination for the Guru. Fascination grows intense of itself due to the effect of the personality of the saint of *Simrin*. One finds in Him the Infinite. And the soul is in perpetual blossom. Mind wanders not and the disciple is one with his Creator."

All enemies, of themselves, become friends; a new adjustment to life comes of itself. Nor does the disciple feel any more inimical with any one. Evil vanishes. To the disciple no more is anything evil. All is good, for he knows the Blissful and the Pure so intimately thenceforward. No more is it he, or I, it is all. 'You, You, the Beloved." The dulling solidity of mind is gone, and fountain-like is the flow of the inspired poet. The presence of the saint and getting to it is all, no other effort is needed in his presence to realize the divine. The Divine is all self-realized. It is spontaneous union. The Eternal song rings in the blood of the disciple and he listens to it with his ears fixed on every pore of his own body. As the lotus opens by the touch of the sun, so no distances can separate man from his God.

The Guru then proceeds to sing an ode to a person of cosmic consciousness—*Brahmgyani*—to one set in Truth, a person like the Lord Buddha.

> He says,—
> "Buddha Himself is God.
> "Unwetted like the lotus by the waters of *Maya*.
> "Shining equally for all, good and bad, low and high, poor and rich, like the sun.
> "Blowing like the breeze as a musical influence for the good of all.
> "A Personality as infinitely patient as the earth; they come and decorate her and the earth endures.
> "This virtue of the *Brahmgyani* is not one of accomplishment, but as spontaneous and as natural, as it is for fire to burn.
> "The *Brahmgyani's* intention is lighted up as is the arched heaven by the suns and the stars.
> "He is the highest type of Personality and is the indweller of the lowliest hearts.
> "They are *Brahmgyanis* whom God hath so made."

As the rose is the rose and mountain, mountain, so this personality of cosmic consciousness is as much an act of the Creator, as the universe itself.

In whose soul, that little kernel of His Name nestles, that man is truly the lover of the Beautiful Lord and his vision is so entranced that he sees not what we see, but sees only his God, his Guru everywhere and in all things. His vision is Beloved-bound. He sees nothing else besides. He has become incapable of seeing the 'other'. This world which is so sordid and dirt-laden is so to the ill-informed eyes. To the man of the Guru, there is another world of his own mind before him. He sees the world that revolves in the Guru's mind. A true devotee is he who is the beloved of God, and is at one with the Creator and not with the created. In that glowing centre, alive and burning, *Karma* does not bind him. He works and has no consciousness left of reaping the harvests that he has sown. Immersed in Naming Him, he is all mercy, all kindness to all.

And he is not only living in that supreme state himself, but wherever he is, he induced the same freedom in others. The saint of *Simrin* is not content with being free himself but is a great liberator of men through his own freedom. The Guru says, he is the true *Pandit* who understands that this solid universe is a vision in the self-consciousness of man, this solid world is in the ethereal 'Unreality' — the world of soul. So this formed universe is more like a dream in that reality. And he is the true philosopher who reconciles all the four castes with the great mystery of the universe, imbues the human soul with the radiance of that shining particle of naming Him. The Guru breathes with the disciple in his breath, and lies, so to say, in bed with him, wakes up with him, and moves with him so does the Guru love His disciples.

Action is all His, no one else acts, so realizes the disciple and is quiet. The Infinite reposes in the Infinite, Glory sleeps in Glory, Glory wakes in Glory.

Living and dying, creation and destruction, saving and destroying, all go as He ordaineth. And the Guru says, the Craftsman sees his own craft as He willeth. His looks are the propellers of all ships. Stones swim on the waters by the threads of His Will, and things live on even if the breath is stopped, such is His miracle! Both this end and that end are in His hands.

The Guru says, "I see no other who acts. He alone is and He alone acts."

"Tell me," says the Guru, "What is, after all, the 'canness' of man. He is driven as He drives."

Man is driven hither and thither and finds no rest. When He so ordaineth, he finds the assonance of the saints *of Simrin* and becomes a steady spiritual entity. Knowledge sprouts up like light in him then and he lives in mansions that do not fade away. He is then dyed in the Divine, deluged with it and he lives with Him, in Him. Thenceforward unmoving like the pole star. That superb state of consciousness is one of the deep confluences, unions, as streams meet streams, as light meets light. All wanderings are over for him, all is realized in this supreme spiritual attitude that knows no trembling away from its centre. Do not found your faith on man, depend not on him, the giver is the Lord Love. Once He gives it to you, you no more thirst for, nor hunger for aught else. Beyond man's power is His saving you or destroying you. God alone dispenses your destinies. By knowing His will you are at rest; seek then, Him and string His Name in the thread of your breath.

Nothing dies, nothing lives, all is His Act.

They who know Him dispel the darkness of disease and pain, "By His favour," says the Guru, "I have found Him and I am at peace." And only those rise and see Him whom He so commandeth. Those whom He calls for His service are the fortunate, glorious persons.

The Guru says, Lord Love is the binder of broken ties. And He sustaineth all souls. He thinks of all, and no one is denied His gifts. Of one's own effort and desire, no one gets to anything. Without Him, all goals of man even when reached are places of despair. The one thing needful is Naming Him.

The beautiful one need not feel vain of his or her beauty, as it is the lustre of love that shines through them. In all hearts, His lamps are burning.

The richness of the rich is His, as the glory of all wealth is glory of Him. The gods laugh at those who sit and think they are givers of gifts when the gifts rain down from Him to everyone. By the Grace of the Guru, the disease of the human 'I' or little self is cured and man attains to the health of his soul.

As the pillar supports the roof of the temple, so the Guru's name supports life. As the stones laden in a boat swim across the river so the disciples living in the Guru cross difficulties. As the light of the burning lamp destroys darkness, so by the touch of the Guru, man's inner-self is lighted. His intention wakes us up to all knowledge. As a benighted traveller in a wilderness finds his way, so the disciple finds the light by kindling his own soul from the burning soul of the saint of *Simrin*.

A naked babe you did enter, O man, here; all was added to you; so why think of all this so petulantly, clutching at shadows and forgetting yourself? What is this moth-like quiver g to death in desire for objects outside yourself? Let your heart beat soundly with His Name and see the world change all its worst aspects for you. You did come for gathering the experiences of the love sensations of 'Naming Him', the thrills of life; you did come for earning your soul; rise and earn it by living in planetary assonance with the soul of the saints of *Simrin*. Wash the flower feet of the saints of *Simrin* and drink. Dedicate yourself to them, keep nothing behind. Bathe in the feet-dust of the Saints. Great fortune falls to them who serve the Saint, and sing the Psalms of the Lord with Him. He, who finds the love of the Guru, obtains faith. Obedience is of the essence of the disciple's worship. The true servant of God is His beloved son and such an inspired servant doth breathe the spirit of 'Naming Him'.

VII

THE 'JAPUJI' OF GURU NANAK

The modern age has been auto-suggesting through its false science of political economy that man lives on bread alone. Miserably small and depressing is this animalistic view of human life. The greatest thinkers of the world have not put faith in bread alone. Pregnant with spiritual beauty are the memorable words of Jesus Christ,—*"Thou shalt not live by bread alone but by every word that proceedeth out of the mouth of God."* All animals get hungry; they must go to the manger, but to glorify this physical necessity, as does the modern world, is the outcome of ignorance and of blindness to spiritual values. My eyes turn upwards and kiss the lotus feet of the Great One who dwells within me when I read the hopeful message,—*"Thou shalt not live by bread alone."* My thirst for reality is greatly assuaged. And when I reflect that Sikhs of the olden time, the disciples of the Guru, lived on the hymn of *'japuji'* I am filled with joy and thankfulness. So profound has been the influence of the constant repetition of this divine lyric by my Sikh ancestors, the ancestry that started only 450 years ago, that when I dip myself in cold water, involuntarily escapes the song out of me as birds cry out at break of dawn. To have dissolved its pure cadences in the blood of the Sikh children is a great artistic work. For this hymn gives joy; it vitalises the whole of our spiritual being, and elevates and ennobles. Its touch cools down all fires of desire and the peace that was the Buddha, comes to the Sikhs to both men and women as they chant the Guru's songs. To-day if you ask any Sikh child to choose between *Japuji* and bread; he will answer unhesitatingly *'Japuji!'* I am glad whenever I find the son of Man rises above physical need. And the true Sikh, a true hero, will not exchange his *Japuji* for the wealth of the three worlds, for the comforts of a Paradise or the joys of a dream-world of intense pleasure. With a broken shoe, a tattered turban, and a thread-bare shirt, a poor toiler on the earth without name or caste reads *Japuji* as he sits clothed in the colour of the false dawn under a tree in the wilderness. His eyes grow red with delight and as he opens them there is the red sun trembling in the east. The Sikh is one with Nature and it is *Japuji* that has brought this about. *Japuji* is a hymn that has in its ring the tremble of the stars, the flickering lamps of this blue-domed Temple. They who live on the surface, rebuke the Sikh for wearing a white turban, but as he raises his head, the clouds disperse and reveal the snow-covered mountain. I sometimes wonder because the mountain is such a splendid Sikh of the Guru. The Sikh copies his fashions of dress from the beautiful in nature. Of what use is life, if my head does not rise above all its circumstances and conditions even as the high white mountain rises above the plains? Seeing the river that comes out of the mountains like a song, is it manly for me to have a heart that is not the fountain of all the rivers that flow? *Japuji* has in it the inimitable rhythm of life in Nature—it makes man a fountain that flows with the milk of human kindness. *Japuji* is the text of the art of living in unison with Nature and with Nature's God. It describes creation, as the divine poet sees it and suggests the realization of cosmic consciousness. Our reasons are of the material and therefore negligible; but feeling is of the spiritual. Nothing in the other scriptures and Bibles of men equals *Japuji* in its wonder, its depth and its simple clarity of perfect revelation of personal truth, Those who have the likeness of God in them dwell within the inmost circle of the family that is Nature. Is it not crude to speak of 'one's own family' and not to be of all families? What is that courtyard which has not the moon and the mountains within its small expanse? What is that house which has not the wondrous expanse of the whole universe? It is miserable to be small. I wonder we do not suffocate in mental misery because of this ignorant exclusiveness. But by its rhythm, *Japuji* of Guru Nanak lifts us up to great heights. We clasp the stars in one hand and the roots of life on earth in the other.

It is a charmed hymn. In its repetition is life. It is wonderful that Guru Nanak resumes his personality in this one hymn of His. We meet the master in its sound. They of this earth have not yet heard of it, but the Heavens resound with its lilt.

I think it is of no benefit to translate it. Having translated it once, in another mood I am impelled to translate it again. At least I wish to translate it endlessly. And it is for ever impossible to translate it. In its vision swing many universes. In its sound live many beautiful gods and goddesses. In its movement there is the thrill of the silver steps of a myriad dancers of the sky. In its repetition is the assonance of a choir of Heaven, and the companionship of the liberated souls. It teaches no philosophy but it imparts the spark of life. Be it true or false, in its chant is the secret of the future esoteric religion of the whole mankind. And one never has enough of this spiritual chant. *Japuji* will make the little sweet intense language of the Punjab the universal language of man. 'A fond hope!' you may say. But love has its ways. And a small track may lead to a new continent I do not know. Love works all miracles. And Guru Nanak's chosen language may, by the love of His name, be the chosen of the people of this earth. Its cadence is audible in Heaven; this much I know.

The 'Japuji' in Brief

O Beloved,
Thy name is Truth.
Thou art the Person who creates,
Thou art the humanity that hath no fear, no enmity.
Thy shining spiritual form is above time and space.
Thou art immortality,
Self-radiant Thou, O Love,
Whom no birth can envisage
And no death can remove.
O Beloved,
Sacred, secret is Thy name,
And it opens like the flower of life in the kindness of the Guru.
Thou art eternity
The beginning Thou,
The middle Thou,
The end Thou.
O Beloved,
Thou art beyond the wings of thought,
Thou art beyond the plumbings of silence.
Without Thee desire is not sated,
And all wise proposings sink with sorrow, nothing avails without Thee.
Living with Thee,
In Thee, O Great Love,
Consenting to be Thine for ever and ever is life's fulfilment.
At the signal of Thy brow
The forms rise,
The souls are cast,
And glory gilds the brow even of the smallest, the meanest.
At the signal of Thy brow
Life is scattered in myriad positions, low and high,
And the souls rise up through pain and pleasure.
Some are the gifted beings in union with Thee

And others wander away, in their orbits, for ever and ever.
All is the superb creation of Thy eyes, O Beloved.
Thou art.
Glory, glory, O Beloved.
All are in Thy sunshine.
Thieves, they say,
Cut-throats, robbers who live on other's blood,
Sinners, slanderers, liars
They say these are mean and small
But when Thou shinest, all is beautiful,
I am attracted out of myself,
Fascinated by Thee I sacrifice myself to Thee,
Glory, glory, O Beloved,
All is well.
Thy palace is of music made,
On its walls the universe breaks in song,
Its sky is full of fair dancers,
The space resounds with the rhythm of soundless bliss,
The rivers and the continents sing Thy Name, O Beloved,
The stars beam with Naming Thee
The mail-clad warrior is fierce,
But his heroic death on the battle-field sings in faint tunes of love Thy anthems of personality-music.
Thy dream rolls on.
Life is inspiration of Thy Beauty,
And they are the princes of Heaven who love, who love,
In that still repose of soul, in the infinite rapture of silence.
When one I buds forth into a million,
When the voices of the rivers become my voice
And the cries of birds on wing my own,
And the leaves of the forest and the blades of grass my myriad tongues,
When one call of mine to Thee, O Beloved, becomes a million, and that million becomes a million again,
And the wheel of the whole Universe moves as a wheel in wheel of song Naming Thee, O Beloved, and ever in harmony with the celestial music within my soul, of Thy Love.
And my once saying "Thou" "Thou", O Beloved, starts the countless ages of life saying "Thou", "Thou".
Of this music is made the ladder that rises up to Thee.
And they meet Thee who scaling this shining ladder cross the frontier.
Beyond, there, up, above, the highest art Thou,
O Beloved,
And higher floats like the nimbus around Thee Thy song of *Nam,*
And the entrance unto Thy Palaces is according to the assonance of one's soul; they enter whom Thou callest,
And the smiths that make men of themselves toil hard at their craft.
They cast and recast their souls in the image of Thee, O Beloved,
From near and far, it is the music of life that ascends to Thee.
Born of waters,
We children of earth
Hear news of Thee from the winds.

Day and night nurse all life.
According to the action of each soul are appointed places for all, be they near or far,
Those who Name Thee, Beloved, are perfected,
Bright are the faces of the victors who have learnt to live in the maddening music of Thy
    Presence. O Love, my Love.

Some of you will say this is not a translation of *Japuji*. True, it is not the million readings we can have of it, but it is one of those readings. Music has an infinite number of moods and meanings. Moreover, this translation is absolutely literal. I should be a blasphemer if I were to give any sense differing from that of the Guru in my translation of His hymns. I like the short rendering given above better than that I gave in 1921 in *The Sisters of the Spinning Wheel*[1] and I still like some of the passages in my earlier version. And when out of the million more renderings I have yet to give in centuries to come, I shall have selected the best, pearl-like in their beauty, and have strung them on a thread of light, I shall then make still other translations and become so vain with pride of wearing the garland, that then perhaps my ambition of translating *Japuji* will have its first crude fulfilment.

I make a personal confession here. I have been saved from death by the love of the maker of *Japuji*. I have doubted frequently with others of the age, the merit of repeating the psalms of the Guru, but by actual experiments conducted by myself on myself, I find that without *Japuji* one dies, that the personal love for the Guru falls into the dust and dirt of daily life and that without *Japuji* one is famished. Without the repetition of the psalm of the Guru one becomes heavy of soul—and knows it not! Repeated singing of the psalm is to me the very essence of the best ethical state of mind. But all lyrical repetition follows love, it cannot precede it. No one who has not learnt the lesson of the sorrow of this life is capable of love of the Guru, and without His love there can be no life of the spirit.

Footnotes:

1. *The Sisters of the Spinning Wheel*, Punjabi University, Patiala, 1976.

VIII

SURTA—SOUL CONSCIOUSNESS

"There is Bliss of Love when *Surta* of the Bridegroom transcending body and mind goes and lives in unison with the *Surta* of the Bride, the Disciple, not otherwise, not otherwise."

—Guru Nana

If soul has not melted into soul, there can be no life of the spirit. Guru Nanak compares the life of the spirit t that of the wedded woman. It is consciousness above body and mind, living in unison with consciousness. All other sc called unisons are illusions on the circumference of the unison in the centres of soul-consciousness.

I have already said that the Guru views the whole history of the human race as the history of new incarnation of Feeling, the One Primeval, the One Ancient that create life. It is the Craftsman worshipping his own craft. And the Guru is interested in human life, in the sensitive soul of it, as expressed in its depression and elevation. This, too, is not a philosopher viewing life, but an artist. To the philosopher, as you know, the restlessness of passion is something undesirable and depression and elevation of soul consciousness is akin to emotional insanity. The philosopher is seeking the equilibrium of the soul, the dead sameness of all things, that is unmoved by pain and pleasure, by cold and heat, by good and evil. Not so, the Guru. Again, the difference between the intellectual and the spiritual self consciousness. The intellectual is confined to its inner self and the spiritual deals with the shining union-points of the inner and the outer soul. Not wholly within, not wholly without, in the rare unison of the two is the Beautiful realized.

Life is indicated, according to the Guru, by the rise and fall of consciousness. *Surta* is the name he gives to the soul or soul-consciousness. Perhaps, you remember the scene in Faust where Margaret expresses to Faust the uncomfortable heaviness she feels pressing on her at the sight of Mephistopheles. Almost protesting against his coming with Faust. That unconscious depression of the *Surta* of Margaret caused by Mephistopheles is deeply interesting to the Guru, it shows that the *Surta* is alive, not petrified, not fossilized. It has the life to bend under depression and to rise up on exhilaration. The true strength is in the sensitiveness, and the true freedom in this freedom of soul-consciousness.

Perhaps you have noticed that wonderful record of the rise and fall of Christ's *Surta* in the Bible.

> "And he that hath no sword, let him sell his garment.
> And he came out and went as he was wont, to the mount of olives, and his disciples followed him.
> And when he was at the place, he said unto them—Pray ye enter not into temptation.
> And he was withdrawn from them about a stone's cast and kneeled down and prayed, saying, Father, if thou be willing remove this cup from me; nevertheless, not my will, but thine, be done.
> And there appeared an angel unto him from Heaven, *strengthening* him.
> And being in agony, he prayed more earnestly
> And his sweat was, as it were, great drops of blood falling down to the ground;
> And when he rose up from praying and was come to his disciples, he found them sleeping for sorrow,

And he said unto them—Why sleep ye? Rise and pray, lest ye enter into temptation,
And while he yet spake, behold! a multitude and he that was called Judas, one of the twelve, went before them and drew near unto Jesus to kiss him.
But Jesus said unto him, Judas, betrayest thou the son of man with a kiss,
When they which were about him saw what would follow, they said unto him, Lord, shall we smite with the sword.
And one of them smote the servant of the high priest and cut off his right ear.
And Jesus answered and said, Suffer ye thus far.
And he touched his ear and healed him."
Mark the state of Christ's *Surta*. How it falls and rises! Christ, in that depression, says:
"And he that hath no sword, let him sell his garment and buy one."

And his *Surta* rises to its normal height and glory when he says, "Suffer ye thus far." And he touched his ear and healed him. In this very scene the condition of the *Surta* of Peter is extremely pitiable:

"And after a little while another saw him and said, Thou art also of them, and Peter said, Man, I am not.
And about the space of one hour after, another confidently affirmed, saying, of a truth this fellow also was with him, for he is a Galilean,
And Peter said, Man, I know not what thou sayest.
And immediately while he yet spake, the cock crew.
And the Lord turned and looked upon Peter. And Peter remembered the words of the Lord, who had said unto him, Before the cock crew, thou shalt deny me then.
And Peter went out and wept bitterly."

This is real biography and most truthful history. The Sikh reads this with interest and he throws away all other history. Nothing else is worth remembering. Peter, too, regains his *Surta* by weeping for the Master restored it by His look. The master had *strengthened* him.

Compare this scene of Christ's life with the scene when he sat in the full effulgence of his God-consciousness:

"And he turned to the woman, and said unto Simon—Seest thou this woman? I entered into thine house, thou gayest me no water for my feet, but she hath washed my feet with tears and wiped them with the hair of her head.
Thou gayest me no kiss, but this woman since the time I came in hath not ceased to kiss my feet.
My head with oil thou didest not anoint, but this woman hath anointed my feet with ointment."
And again when he says:
"And Jesus said unto them; I am the bread of life, he that cometh to me shall never hunger and he that believeth in me shall never thirst.
I am the light of the world, he that followeth me shall not walk in darkness but shall have the light of life."

And how glorious is the saying of this God, the Son speaking as the Father:

"For the poor always ye have with you but me ye have not always."

In his elevated *Surta,* Christ felt like a divine Bridegroom which indeed he was. The following is the tribute paid by a sorrow-stricken man to such God-consciousness:

> "And, above all, Christ is the most supreme of individualists. It is the man's soul that Christ is always looking for. He calls it 'God's Kingdom' and finds it in everyone. He compares it to little things, to a tiny deed, to a handful of leaven, to a pearl.
>
> "That is because one realizes one's soul only by getting rid of all alien passions, all acquired culture, and all external possessions, be they good or evil.
>
> "People have tried to make him out an ordinary philanthropist or have ranked him as an altruist with the unscientific and sentimental. But he was really neither the one nor the other. Pity he has, of course, for the poor, for those who are shut up in prisons for the lowly, for the wretched, but he has far more pity for the rich, for the hard hedonists; for those who waste their freedom in becoming slaves to thing, for those who wear soft raiment and live in kingly house~ Riches and pleasures seemed to him to be greater tragedies than poverty and sorrow. To live for others with a definite self-conscious aim was not his creed. It was not the basis of his creed. When he says, 'Forgive your enemies', it is not for the sake of the enemy, but for one's own sake that he says so and because love is more beautiful than hate. In his entreaty to the young man, 'Sell all thou hast and give to the poor,' it is not of the state of the poor that he is thinking but of the soul of the young man, the soul that wealth was marring.
>
> "For, I see in Christ not merely the essentials of the supreme romantic type, but all the accidents, the wilfulness even of the romantic temperament also. He was the first person who ever said to the people that they should live 'flower-like lives.' He fixed the phrase. He took children as the type of what people should try to become."
>
> "Dante describes the soul of a man as coming from the hand of God 'weeping and laughing like a little child.'
>
> "He felt that life was changeful, fluid, active and that to allow it to be stereotyped into any form was death.
>
> "He said that people should not be too serious over material common interests; that to be impractical was to be a great thing, that one should not bother too much over affairs. The birds did not, why should man? He is charming when he says 'Take no thought for the morrow; is not the soul more than the raiment? Is not the body more than the raiment?'
>
> "His morality is all sympathy, just what morality should be. His justice is all poetical justice, exactly what justice should be. The beggar goes to Heaven because he has been unhappy.
>
> "Like all poetical natures he loved ignorant people. He knew that in the soul of one who is ignorant there is always room for a great idea. But he could not stand stupid people, especially those who are made stupid by education, people who are full of opinions not one of which they can understand.
>
> "Mary Magedelene when she sees Christ, breaks the rich vase of perfume that one of her seven lovers had given her and spills the odorous species over his tired dusty feet and for that one moment's sake, she sits for ever with Ruth and Beatrice in the tresses of the snow-white rose of Paradise. All that Christ says to us by way of a little warning is that every moment should be beautiful, that the soul should always be ready for the coming of the Bridegroom, always waiting for the voice of the lover, philistinism being, simply, that side of man's nature that is not illumined by imagination."

To me this is not the praise of Christ, but it is a brilliant description of the *Surta* that Christ had. It is the description of elevated inspired *Surta*. It is as the Guru says the Guru—'the Bridegroom'—Personality Impersonal. The *Guru* is impersonal because He is Buddha, Christ, and He is without body and yet with an eternal body that is the medium of the radiation of the Guru personality.

Ye Sikh young men! some of you are longing to have what they call an authentic history of the Sikhs. And you do not realize that the only authentic history for such as you is the putting together of the minutest details of the experiences of the soul, the sensitive soul, which only a spiritual genius can write. You need the experimental truths of the rise and fall of your soul-consciousness. Possibly, the Faust of Goethe is a better Sikh history, in this sense, than anything you can write. The rise and fall of *Surta* as recorded in the New Testament is the history of the whole man, the holy man. The tired intellect of man, the blinded eye of his, will one day realize that the biography of Christ as in the New Testament is the only right type of biography. The other kind is a lie, is vanity that sickens the soul. Intellectual interpretations exhaust genius, it is self-spending of consciousness. Unless you watch the lotus of self-consciousness close and open and unless you have the sensitiveness of a sensitive plant, you have not yet entered the Realm of Right Information.

1. This Divine Lamp

The Guru is not concerned with what we do and eat, what we speak and think; those who call attention to these details do not yet know of the one thing needful. He only enquires, in what state is your *Surta*? —And where? Is it whole? Is it on the heights of glory? or depressed? And is it delicately poised so as to be sensitive to the inspiration from the High? Is man like a lyre that shall sing when the breezes from that Great Region blow all unawares? We, as Sikhs, shall read the human history even in fiction as the Guru intends. A poor Mussalman says that Guru Nanak never visited Mecca as if his visiting Mecca cannot take place in our brain. His visit to the Mecca is only required by us to learn that God whom they, the. Moslems, say is in Kaaba is everywhere. It is only to correct a human misconception, otherwise the Mecca is as good a city as any other in the desert dotted with palms. The Beduins are no better men than the Mussalmans of Malabar.

The conqueror's *Surta* finds an elevation in conquests, but what is the state of the conqueror when defeated? There is a smell of it in the amorous love of man for woman but what when she rejects him? There is a glow of *Surta* in finding sudden material prosperity surrounding one but what when it all goes away? In everyday life, we sink and soar with the non-fulfilment or fulfilment of our desires. And, according to the Guru, the true education of man is his self-study of *Surta* to attain to heights and to maintain them and to gather greater and greater strength in his *Surta*. It is, as Guru Nanak says, the craftsman's toiling on his craft. It is the slow growth by a continuous active silence. This strength of *Surta* is not like the strength of muscle, or of steel. It is the strength of the poet's imagination. It is intensity that burns and whose light no darkness can dim. It is, as Guru Gobind Singh says, a light burning all the twenty-four hours in the temple of our heart. And the greatest strength of *Surta* is not in itself but in its attunement with its spiritual atmosphere which is redolent with the presence of music of the invisible Helpers. Truly is it written, "And there appeared an angel unto him from Heaven *strengthening* him." Mark the word *strengthening* him; *him* is Christ himself here. The strength of *Surta* is the strength of faith. When St. Paul on the shipwreck assured the doubting Roman soldiers that they would be all saved as Christ had appeared to him and told him of it, it was a natural phenomenon of strengthening the disciple's *Sutra*. The phenomenon is of no consequence as related, but the fact of Paul being strengthened with some unique kind of inspiration is glorious.

Surta is the thread which keeps us linked with the spiritual realms of which Guru Gobind Singh speaks so wondrously. He says:

> "I did not desire to come down from there,
> But He wished and I came;
> But my *Surta* is still pierced with the Remembrance of His Lotus Feet."

And all life is strung like beads on the same thread. Hate not, for the thought of hatred makes your *Surta* muddy. Remember no injury done to you, for any such harbouring of ill-feeling affects your *Surta* adversely. Be not of small heart, narrow mind, contrite, miserly, miserable, for it contracts, your *Surta*. Like the sky and the stars be infinite of heart, broad as the earth, large as the sea, a giver and not a beggar, because all these things create an atmosphere of inspiration for your *Surta*. "Remember the Great one," says Guru Nanak. Pour these sparks of love into the vase of your *Surta*. Fill it with beauty. Slowly, gradually, fill it. Fill it with the gladsome lyrical silence of years of your life, till oceans of joy roll out of you. Subtle, indeed, is the sensitive balance of *Surta*.

As a musician cannot stand a harsh note, so a man of *Surta* cannot stand souls that are heavy with desire.

He can live with ignorant people who cast no shadows on him, but it is suffocating for him to live with men of opinions, the heavy ones whose flesh smells of prudence, plans, and rottenness of mind. Even if they are, what people say 'Pure', such are heavy.

A gift of a few parched grains coming out of the spontaneous feeling of offering to God from a prostitute will be welcome to a man of *Surta*, but a garland of pearls from a heavy soul will, when put on his neck with all the outward show of worship, bite him like a snake. His neck would begin to burn with the defilement and corruption of the man making such a present.

Sister Nivedita records what Shree Ram Krishan Parmahansa used to say about things offered to him and left on his mat. To some he would say, "Take away, take away, some one has polluted my mat." To others, "I can eat this; some good soul has offered me this." This sensitive respect for feelings divine that make the human breast pure, is highly aesthetic. In fact, no one but the man of the highest *Surta* can be so sensitive. Such is the highest aestheticism of the sensitive soul.

One day, I saw a man bringing the best almonds as an offering to a man of *Simrin*. He was socially, as they say, "A big man." But his almonds had the odour of thick darkness, they smoked of meanness, smallness of soul. The Faqir had all of them thrown out of his window to the rivers. All the Pundits, celibates, ascetics and holy ones who waited for Rama Chandra were heavy with purity, and. Shibiri, the Bhil woman, in her lowliness, was brighter than they. When Rama Chandra reached there, they all complained that the pond of drinking water had become bitter, and that it was infested with worms and they prayed that he may bathe his holy feet in the water so that it might become sweet and fresh again. And Rama Chandra, they say, bathed his feet therein, but there was no change in the water. They prayed again. And Rama Chandra replied, "Not me, that Bhil woman has that elevation of soul at this moment. Your water has gone bitter because of your purity. You think she is low-caste. Invite her to wash her feet in your pond. And the water will be fresh and sweet." Rama Chandra was the knower of the states of *Surta,* the Pundits, as always, were blind like stones. The despised Bhilini bathed her feet and the pond became sweet again! Such is the miracle of an elevated *Surta*. If anyone is to attempt to write the history of the Sikhs, it should be from the viewpoint of this omniscience that records the effects of men and things. It is no use repeating dull material and so-called moral stories! Rama Chandra saw the spiritual elegance of Bhilini. Without that sensitive omniscience, who dare write Sikh history? Only fools concern themselves with what they call historical events. The greatest events are of the soul and they are revealed in one's own *Surta*. The higher it flies, the deeper it knows the truth of life. Prahalad's *Surta* is always singing, dancing. But when the red hot pillar is before him and he is asked to embrace it, like Christ he calls, "Father, if thou be willing, remove this cup from me". This trembling of *Surta* shows that the *Surta* is alive.

The petrified *Surta* may seem to be strong but it is not alive. And generally the *Surta* of those, who, like the Pharisees and Jews, love money and cant, is dead. Generally, the theological atmosphere dulls the brilliance of the soul. When there is no stir in you at the sunrise, when you leap not forward to meet God in nature and man, when you lead dull, listless lives, then your *Surtas* are dead. And generally dead are the *Surtas* of the professional priests and preachers. That *Surta* is alive which is alive with the spirit of love.

> "And peerless is their beauty who have got embedded in their *Surta* a small grain of inspiration." —*Sukhmani*

2. THE SPIRITUAL UNIVERSE AT THE BACK OF THE MAN OF SPIRIT WHO IS AUTHORISED

Surta, as conceived by the Guru, has the companionship and personality of legions. 'I'—'will'—'volition' is only one and when it advances out on venture as in the case of Caeser, Alexander and Napoleon, it drops in a miserable depression, being single. All such 'I's' not informed of the legions behind, feel that their rear is cut and they are let adrift as kites in the mid sky. And *Surta* is that 'I' which has at its back the whole Heaven. 'I' on earth registers the power of Heaven and its performances are miracles and are the only true historical events for the development of the soul. The whole *Ramayana* is beautiful because it is characterisation of *Ahankara,* with the 'I' cut off from the legion as of Ravana and 'I' bound with the legion as of Rama Chandra. Neitsche confuses the elevation of the *Surta* with the legion, with the elevated ego or the swelling of 'I' as of the Pharaohs of Egypt. Man is superman when his *Surta* has seen its rear and is bound with it through inspiration. And few supermen have there been in the history of man. The superman is only a state of *Surta;* it cannot be on the same level always. The superman is a state of consciousness, not a person. And the superman is but a mean tyrant when he sees not his rear but advances to his doom on the skulls of men. Shiva is the picture of *Surta,* so powerful like death itself, yet dances with the joy of the life of the whole universe. No great dreams can be at all impersonal, they must have shape and colour.

Weakness is the fact of being alone in this universe, however full of strength be the arms of such a weak man. The day comes when the winds blow west when he asks them to blow east, and gold becomes dust when he touches it, though, only a while ago, the dust turned into gold when he touched it. He seeks the aid of friends and friends, he finds, are his foes. Everything turns against him, while, a while ago, all was so friendly. This is weakness. Napoleon in St. Helena was never a strong man, for if he ever were a strong man, he would have made St. Helena itself a paradise on this earth. People would not have remembered the victory of Waterloo, but the victory of the dweller of St. Helena. The Victory of Solitude, of the Silence of Soul. St. Helena would have been another Mecca. Jesus did not win in the Napoleonic sense. He was defeated, they spat at him while alive. He was given a big cross to bear. But what has been the glory of Jerusalem? Compare Jerusalem and St. Helena. Such is the difference between the strength that is inwardly and essentially a weakness and weakness that is inwardly and essentially a strength. Neitsche builds, in some confusion of ideas, his Superman with the millionfold strength of a Napoleon, of an Alexander or a Caesar, but his Superman is then like a mountain which is the food of rain and snow and wind and lightning.

The Guru also invokes a Superman, a strong man. But it is the strength of a continuous link with the legion beyond or behind or in man. It is the strength of Remembrance, of *Simrin*. "Not I, but He fights for me," said Phula Singh. Like a child, he prayed when the numerous hordes of the Pathans besieged him at Saido. It was a prayer to no unseen God. Guru Gobind Singh, the king of legions, was beside and the disciple called to him. The Sikhs won that day a spiritual victory. They were a handful. And the Pathans, it is reported, say that that day each one of the Pathans saw that he was surrounded by ten Phula Singh-like Sikhs wearing broad sleeved blue shirts and long blue cony turbans of the Akalis, shouting '*Akal, Akal*'. Phula Singh Nihang could multiply himself by a word. This is truly the feature of the consciousness of the *Surta* of. a Superman. Such events in themselves are very trite looking. Saido might have been a Waterloo such hundreds there are. But the flash in those common clouds is for us all important and that flash is all important for all seekers of God or the Personal Truth.

They, the Saints, they say, have condemned, *Ahunkar*, 'I,. But the Guru says 'I' is the cure of the disease 'I'. It is by 'I' that 'I' is transcended. There is no other way. When it becomes one with the legion, it is transcended. The white 'I' of the lotus abloom on its stem is beautiful, how can the 'I' of man be ugly? Only it is besmeared with the sin of isolation from the all. It needs being washed in an infinitude. From this axial bud of life, this, 'I', grows the whole tree of life. We have to make it as beautiful and as delicate as a flower. When 'I' becomes beautiful, it ceases to be 'I'. But then there are many charming superstitions by which, the broken 'I's are made whole. I was lying in bed for months, they say of illness. I now see of broken *Surta,* and there was no cure. I was dying. A man brought me an apple, it was a red Cashmere apple. I ate it and I was as if never ill. The apple had in its juice the wishes of a Saint of *Simrin* that I should be whole again. I seldom go to the Golden Temple at Amritsar, but once, after long, when He took me there, I felt I entered a Realm I had never seen before. My forehead touched the sacred marble of that Floor of Wonder and my soul left this earth. For years I thought I was His, but, that night, I saw I never was His till that moment. I was only imagining I was His, the real sensation of being His came to me only then by a dark-night visit to the Golden Temple. At the touch of the marble floor my soul mounted up. When one falls, it is possible one may not know for months and years where one is fallen or whether one is fallen at all; but when he meets some surprise of love again, and he is brought out of the pit, he then feels to what degradation he had slipped all so unconsciously and remained there when all the while he was feeling that he was in a beautiful state, but he was not. You might have noticed that we eat every day and we bathe every day and for years we feel it is all right, but one day we eat as we never ate before, we bathe as we never bathed before, and we feel pleasure as we never felt before. All this difference awakens us to ourselves and we sleep again. With most of us it is sleeping the long sleep and after years to wake for a moment and see that we had forgotten the lesson of the Guru. But to the more developed it is supersensitiveness. They fly away from a priest, and they stand for hours by a courtesan, looking at her. Not that they hate the one or love the other in any particular sense, but only that by such an eccentric act they feel well. Rigidity of any kind tends to poison the *Surta*. *Sutra* is life, and stereotyped routine or the rigidity of any opinions or principles tends to petrify it. Even the codified morality of categorical imperatives is deadening. Therefore, a man of *Surta,* as I have referred to above, is like life 'changeful, fluid, active.' Guru Arjun Dev says, "He who cannot melt himself into tears, tears of bliss and sympathy and thankfulness, how can he enter the kingdom of Heaven? The man of *Surta* has no patience with the dull lifeless mechanical system that treats people as if they were things and treats everybody alike. The man of *Surta* is the supreme artist as distinguished from a metaphysician. He has a highly developed aesthetic individuality. And as the poet thinks that the world is there 'to lend me a metaphor,' the Sikh has it that the world is there, 'to lend me a thrill, a sensation of the Beautiful to raise my *Surta* up to wave in the air with the self-spirituality of a fully blown lotus waving on its stem.'

The life of the Spirit, according to Guru Nanak, is a gift of Heaven, it is the bestowal of authority upon some one sent into this dark world as a torch-bearer. A tiny small man who has been so *authorized* can, if he chooses, bestow genius, comfort of soul and love upon any one. He can forgive sins, he can destroy the dark past by calling the whole energy of the angels into operation. The life of the spirit can bestow freedom on slaves of illusion and make the miserable Kings of the Three worlds at peace, as happy as a poor man, and make the poor man as happy in himself as if he were King of the whole universe.

IX

THE SWORD OF GURU GOBIND SINGH

Every Sikh is to wear His Sword. Not his own. *Kirpan* is a gift from the Guru. It is not an instrument of offence or defence; it is mind made intense by the love of the Guru. The Sikh is to have a sword-like mind. It is the visible sign of an intensely sensitive soul.

The sword cuts so rapidly, the mind can do so much in an instant. That common herd mentality with its drolly dullness, with utter incapacity to fly like the Eagles of Heaven cannot live together with the sword of Guru Gobind Singh. It is but the symbol of the myriad personality of the Guru's Sikh, that knows no defeat, no disappointment, the personality, that is unconquerable in its hope, in its spiritual radiance. Guru Gobind Singh says, "I will make my one dominate over a million." This domination is of the illumined mind. The highly intensified and developed intellect naturally becomes overpowering, so much so that it becomes fascinating and attractive in a physical sense. It gathers its own moths like the intense flame of a night lamp. The presence of a great spiritual man overpowers millions. What is mind if it has not the flash of the lightning and the sword? All conquests in the fields of life are mental and moral; physical conquests are no conquests. I think he who wears the Guru's sword, is a spontaneous man fully grown in His spirit and is of His Spirit. This is to say a great deal. Herd mentality wearing Guru's sword is as great a mockery as the lighting of oil lamp in brass plates before the stone idol of Jagan Nath, against which Guru Nanak sang his famous *Arti*. It is no use wearing His Sword, if one has not become wholly spiritual and the animal in man has not shrunk to a pretty pet or, as St. Francis said, "his ass" or the forgotten shadow of a byegone self.

When He touched my hair and blessed me, how could I bear my hair being shorn? The Sikh is the dedicated. I nestle the fragrance of His touch in my tresses. I am the bride. They, of the modern era, have bobbed the bride but the Sacred Braids of Christ still remain the most beautiful adornment of man's or woman s head. I love the Guru s superstition. The lightning spark is concealed in the wool of the wandering cloud in the sky and the life spark of the Guru. is hidden in this sheaf of hair. They say it is troublesome to carry it. But more troublesome is a life of no inspiration. The body itself is not less troublesome. The daily toilet, powder and puff and rogue, and pearlcaps, and arranging of ear drops and shingles is in no way less troublesome. And when one is reconciled to such a thing as the human body, to such a thing as this impossible life, it is emptiness of soul, it is bankruptcy of love for God and for the Guru to think of the riddance of hair, the spiritual crown of humanity. The modern woman, as I have said elsewhere, has lost most of her soul by shingling her hair and puffing an odorous reed in her rose-bud-like lips.

I heard a stupid Sikh preacher the other day, trying to convince a mass gathering of the Sikhs that the iron ring of the Guru worn on the wrist is a protection against lightning. He said, as large buildings are made safe against lightning by a rod of iron, so the Guru has saved man from the stroke of lightning. He was hopelessly flinging his arms up and down to gather some straw of a reason to prove the rationale of the iron ring the Guru gave us as a gift. Coming to us from our personal God, dearer to us than our mother, father, sister or sweetheart, it comes to us as His Gift, as His Blessing. Fie on Our manners that we argue over and over about it. He touched my hair and I keep it; when I toss my arm up in the air and the iron ring shines, I am reminded of His wrist that wore it—one exactly like this. Is this arm, by some stray gleam of the iron ring on my wrist, His? Other religions live in an elaborated symbolism; I the Sikh have no religion. He loved me, He made me His own. The sword is the mind where the Guru lives. The iron ring is the sign of His remembrance. The tresses of hair are as clouds round a snow peak—

they always gather, gather—they always rain, rain. In my sacred tresses flow Ganga, Jamna and Godavari. Have I got the comb, the Guru gave me? Have I got His other gifts? I may have lost them. But I cannot lose my tresses, I cannot lose my iron ring. Because, you remember how He called His disciple Bhai Gurdas from Benares. The disciples went as bidden and brought him with his hands bound with a string from Benares to Amritsar. Once the call of the Master was answered thus. Each one of us is called. We are of His Spiritual militia. We have to wear the ring which is His gift, and we are the prisoners of infinite love. These are the fetters of love, the price of our freedom. Each Sikh wears hair and the beard of Guru Gobind Singh. We are moulded in His image.

Those who do not have that great personal love for the Guru are still out of court. But our freedom is in Him and not anywhere without Him. Do not talk to us in that strain of the Sikh preacher. These are not the symbols of a religion, nor essential rites of any religious discipline. They are the signs of our being 'wedded women'. They are the wedding gifts from the Bridegroom. He gave all these to us, and they are sacred. Superstitious? Yes. But which love hath not and where at all hath love not its own superstitions?

X

INTERNATIONALISM AND THE SIKHS

The Sikhs are creations of Guru's universal love. They are by their very birth of His spirit, citizens of the world.

This small world has been knitted together now as never before. Though wars still rage and will rage, for brothers must fight for patrimony, the spirit of fraternal reconciliation is in the air. Blood is thicker than water, and of the same wheaten bread and water and grapes and salt and wine we make the scarlet blood. The human body is one. The human soul is one. Human beauty is one. Our perception of the Beautiful is one; our self-intoxication is the same. Our pursuits of pleasure are alike. There is no difference between man and man. Our Guru says, the ears, the eyes, the speech of man are the same all the world over. The Guru also traces the angelic and the divine in us and emphasises this feature of our nature, showing how we may indistinguishably mingle with the angels in the Realm of angels. The heart-beat of man is alike from Japan to America, and man has already begun to recognize his heart-beat in all living things. Abraham Lincoln's fight for the freedom of slaves in America gives him the dignity of a prophet amongst statesmen. That large sympathy of man for man is the recognition of the same heart-beat. Men, few men, have gone further, some for brief moments of inspiration, others for long, and they feel their blood in the veins of the animals. Buddha prohibited animal slaughter. Priyadasa issued edicts which made the beef-eating Aryan races of India vegetarian. This was the mass appreciation of Tathagatha's great compassion for all sentient beings. The society for the prevention of cruelty to animals is typical of the curious contradiction of the nature of the man who eats chicken with his plate of rice and goes out of doors to prosecute a driver who is beating mercilessly with his lash his jaded horse in order to get a little more speed out of him. Wars rage and sisters of mercy nurse the wounded of both camps. All these contradictions of feeling only show that something nobler is stirring in the human mind and soon it will be born.

The universal brotherhood of man has become a cant from the lips of the priest, as the universal oneness of life from the lips of the philosopher. All the higher tendencies of civilized and cultured men tend towards universal kinship. All desire peace upon the earth, this small sweet home of man. The days of patriotism are gone; patriotism was a foolish clannishness. In these days man with a patriotic feeling is a brute, because patriotism makes him blind to the larger interest of the family of man. All the barbaric selfishness that still dominates the narrow-minded politics of the Governments of different countries is due to the wrong notion '*This for me alone and for none else.*' We need not recall here the stupid jealousy of the white settlers in different parts of the world who reserve the best pieces of land and the best rights of man for themselves and look with manifest contempt on the coloured races. For that jealousy is the rotten patriotism of the old world when brother was divided from brother and neighbour waged war against neighbour. We need not refer to the strength of arms that crushes the low-lying victim and eats it up, for there are men who have not yet been able to rise above man-eating tendencies. We need not refer to the fight that is going on apace all over the world between capital and labour, the aristocratic state and the proletariat, for this strife only thickens the gloom before us. The gloom of centuries seems to thicken still in the old ways of the brute and the beast. We, however, wish to look at the distant rays of the coming Dawn of Peace between brother and brother, members of the one human family.

In the modern world, there is no towering personality, the race of the old worthies has been run. England has not yet given us another Carlyle nor America produced another Abraham Lincoln. And because of this want of greatness, there is confusion not only in the direction of world-politics but in all human affairs. Little points that Napoleon would have solved as part of the day's work, are put before committees and sub-committees and take years of discussion and still remain the fourteen points unsolved.

This is the misfortune of modem times. Great men are true representatives of the people. So they have been in all ages, for true greatness is always representative. But the giants are gone, and now the tiny dwarfs flutter and shake their wings. They have not the soul in them to take any responsibility. They are not great enough. They have misunderstood democracy. By the introduction of the idea of democracy into politics, perhaps, that tall, Himalayan kind of human personality has been made impossible. All have become sand grains in one great level desert. The winds blow and heaps of sand are gathered here and there and then are blown away. Such is the fate of human affairs in this age—a significant fate! All ideals are in the melting pot and from the great liquid will crystallize the New Ideals. Then the world being tired of these dwarfs will cry for its old Himalayan giants again. *"Down with democracy!"* will they cry, as they once cried *"Down with Kingship."* There will be no revolutions, for revolutions have not made us a bit more comfortable than the old obedience. Better obedience. At present, we can only see the tendencies. One great bent of human thought is towards internationalism. And I dare say this thought began in the modern world with Guru Nanak. *"Down with caste distinctions!"* Man is one. There is no such thing as Hindu or Sikh or Mohammadan or Christian, the eastern or the western. Man is man, and man is one. As long as man carries a label distinguishing him from his brother man, he has not risen to the dignity of man. True culture is that which does not make him a Sikh, or Mohammadan or Hindu or Christian, but a man. True education is that which does not make him Indian or English or Japanese or American but a man. A truly educated and cultured man is he whose radiant sympathy, whose genuine feelings, whose brilliant mind, whose God-like manners bring him the spontaneous kinship of all the races of man Wherever he may go, so that he becomes indistinguishably a man of all countries, colours, climes and castes. This is the spirit of the Gurus. Guru Nanak fascinated Mardana. Mardana never after seeing him called himself a Mohammadan. Bhai Nand Lal after seeing Guru Gobind Singh never called himself a Hindu. Whosoever met the Guru in his soul said *"He was no other but a man."* There is one sky over a Mohammadan's, a Hindu's, a Christian's head; the same winds blow for everyman, for everyman the same waters flow. When the river has no such labels, it is gross ignorance to call ourselves Hindus, Mohammadans, Sikhs, Christians—and there are many others—names which divide rather than knit us together. Of what use is our going to the prophets and saying we are their followers, if we are a disgrace to their genius, genius which was exhausted by making the human wolves flock together as lambs under the protection of one shepherd? When the Guru says man is one, it is blasphemy for us to recognize Hindus, Mohammedans and Christians any more. Bhai Bir Singh of the Sikh time is the type of the Guru's man. He lived in a Fort, he was of the Guru. Though a man of renunciation, he lived like a king in a fort, such is the need of the soul that is given to the Guru. He had minstrels to sing to him, for they loved to see him grow translucent in flesh as they sang and loved to see that tears of ecstasy roll down from his closed eyes on his cheek, as a baby weeping in his cradle in dream. They said he had more of Him than they had, so they sang to him, they recognized him as their price. And the Fort was a temple in the image of the Golden Temple of the Guru. The herd of Sikh soldiery mad with lust of revenge on the men and princes who opposed their mob rule besieged the Fort of Baba Bir Singh. "Either surrender such and such a Sikh prince who has taken refuge in the Fort or we blow it up." The ultimatum was given. "My fort? No, it is the Temple of Guru Nanak. The prince has taken shelter with the Guru. I am nobody here. All right, let them blow us up."

The mad soldiery started the firing.

"Come, ye minstrels, and sing now our wedding song," said the old saint whom the religious history of the world does not know, because the Guru's man never proclaims himself. Loving the rapturous silence of His Love he lives and dies in it. "My system is for me to live by. And I am as a tree that gives shade wherever I am." And the minstrels came and gathered round him. They began singing the psalms of the Guru. The shells fell. That rampart is gone, that parapet is broken. And then fell a shell in the choir and the Baba was gone. But before this happened, the inmates of the fort asked his permission to reply fire, for they had all fire-arms and ammunition. "No," said the Baba. "They are brothers, not enemies." "But they are firing." "They know not we are their brothers. We know they are. This knowledge makes all the difference." The difference was death. For those who value the Guru's ideal of brotherhood prefer death. There is indeed no justification for the man of the Guru to hate any sentient thing, far less a man. It is therefore no fanatic thought of a fervent Sikh that this ideal of the brotherhood of man starts with the Guru. This one great tendency of the modern epoch of the world of internationalism has its root in the ideals of the Guru. These ideals put you to shame. You are not amongst yourselves full of pure love for each other, you have not yet dropped selfishness in love and given yourselves wholly to love. In face of this small performance, your calling yourselves His only is empty talk. But we must hang our heads in shame and stand condemned, if we have not yet acknowledged love as the only substance of human life. It is not for me to remind you of your performance. I am showing you how in the modern world the idea of the Guru is slowly appearing as softly and as brightly as the morning sun embroiders with a thin ribbon of gold the black velvet of the winter clouds. We have not yet risen to His Ideal. We are not His yet, in spite of wearing two swords and two turbans and drinking the sugared syrup to our heart's content. Self-flattery cannot give us wings to fly. Those who have wings fly and never see the earth. The larks know naught but their own song.

The second great tendency of the modern world is towards dropping the so-called religions. Enough of them. The world is tired of them. And I call your attention to this, this very disgust of the Guru, the disgust of a well-informed, fully-emancipated mind of the modern age apparent m every page of the Guru's writings. If you read closely *Asa-di-Var,* you will find it. If you read *Akal Ustat* of Guru Gobind Singh you will find it, indelibly written. All gods are relegated to the past. All religions are thrown away. If you look at the type of lives the Guru created in the Punjab, you will for the first time see the Ideals of civic life coming into being. You will see men with families serving the poor and the weak with their very lives. A man apparently not of their persuasion comes complaining to the Sikhs assembled in the Golden Temple at Amritsar that a tyrant has snatched away his wife. The assembled men all rise and go. Some of them die in the affray, others restore the wife to her husband. These were men wholly unpractical in the ordinary worldly prudent sense. They recked not of power and of the kingdoms of this world. For all belong to the Guru, we are his dedicated servants. This feeling made the men of the Guru as universal as wind and river and light. If our daily life is not ideal as was that of the old disciples of the Guru's, if we have no spiritual expression of the Guru's ideal in our society, and in our homes, if there is no musical peace of the soul as expressed, say in the homes of artistic Kyoto or Tokio, nay more, if there is not more cleanliness, more divine human feeling, more spiritual charm that fascinates us in the aesthetic Japanese, in the temples and offices of the Shiromani Gurdwara Prabandhak Committee, then of what use is our falling flat with both our arms spread on the floor of our temple and of what use is our cry to possess them? Then I will frankly call this possession of temples by my *Akali* brothers a bearish embrace of brick and mortar. If the spirit of the Guru which alone makes all temples sacred has departed from our hearts, of what interest to us or to the world are our shrines? If our shrines do not establish an atmosphere of that inner music which rained down from the thorny branches of the Punjab acacia when Brother Lehna shook it under the bidding of Guru Nanak and the hungry were fed, the significance of shrines to a people so lost to love and passionate love of the Guru's perfection shrinks to nothingness. And the superstitions and formal sanctimonious regard for them is the sign of the death of that feeling which brought them into existence. I am for the absolute maintenance of the spiritual atmosphere, but not for that exclusive possession as of our peculiar inherited property. I see no reason why in the Golden Temple should not gather the Hindu and the Moslem and the Christian to recite their *kathas* and songs, provided they serve to maintain the peaceful, radiant spiritual atmosphere characteristic of the Guru's teaching. That great calm harmony of the complexity of faith and the inner oneness of all religions is the special theme of the Gurus. The very first thinker on comparative religion was Guru Nanak. Akbar followed in a weak dreamy way, obsessed with the sense of his being an Emperor and capable of starting a new religion. Abul Faizi perhaps was responsible for his doings. The modern world East and West followed. The great spirit of 'toleration for all religions that modern religious movements such as Theosophy have started, the unifying cultural movements of the world, are all under the driving *sankalpa* of the Guru whose mind governs the activities of the coming world that is to take shape according to His will. In fact, there were many Hindus who had staunch devotion for the Sikh ideals. True they did not join us, but they had sympathy with our persuasion and we have thrown them out. Our Guru says, "I embrace the sweeper who has His *Nam* in him." And we shut the doors of our heart. The shutting of temple doors is immaterial, but the shutting of the doors of the heart is not in harmony with the Guru's ideal of the universal kinship of man. People point out that we do not treat the low castes that have joined (perhaps only outwardly for social reasons) our persuasion on a basis of human equality. The sad fact is not our treatment of these people, but the smallness of our moral stature in comparison with the ideals of the Guru. Closely connected with this comes the question of what they are pleased to call "our symbols". We as men of the Guru have no symbols. We, I say, as men of the Guru have no so-called religion or religious creed as others have. "Then what are these impediments of long hair and heard?" asks the impatient young Sikh who sees that the whole world is clean-shaven with a cigarette in its lips. And it is so neat looking. "I wish to be like that. After all what does the hair matter when my heart is pure?" The question is quite simple to answer when the answer is based on an intellectual analysis of things. And who is there to compel any one to be of the Guru, unless one feels the need of His love and His protection and His Ideal and unless one seeks ardently for Him?

But those who have been to Him and have loved Him and have received His gifts cannot throw the gifts of the Guru to the winds and still say they love Him. It is a question of the intensity of personal love for the Guru. Those braids of Jesus Christ and these sacred knots of the Five Beloved of Guru Gobind Singh who tied them on their heads with his own hands are His Gifts thenceforward. For one who has any feeling in his breast, death is more welcome than parting with His gifts. But at the same time, we should not be so foolish as to impose the possession of these gifts as a condition on the modern man for his capacity to *sympathize* with the Guru's ideals and to accept them for his soul. As I told you, I feel it is the Guru's ideals that are working in the world to-day and the shape and colour and race and religion of the different nations of the earth do not hinder the growing acceptance of those ideals. Men are driven to go Guru-ward. All the modern tendencies, political and religious, are turning men towards Him. It is simply stupid in this age of the progressive tendencies of man to tie him down to any superstitious symbols. Symbols will be discarded if they are merely symbols. But we Sikhs of the Punjab saw Him, met Him. He gave us His personal love and we gave Him ours, though we went astray and still go astray. The sacred knot of hair is our veritable crown, because it is His gift. Better death than parting with this gift. After a short while, except for this shape of the Guru, all other things they call symbols shall be as one chooses. To say that because a Punjabi Sikh binds a turban, the American Sikh sympathiser shall therefore be precluded from wearing his hat is the idle jugglery of an ignorant fanaticism for a local personal gratefulness to Him who freed us from caste and superstition and saved us from the hands of political tyrants. But different indeed shall be the covering of one who meets Guru Gobind Singh and gets a particular headwear as a gift. You all remember how Guru Amar Das during his discipleship received from Guru Angad Dev a piece of *khaddar* as a gift and token of His love for him. The disciple knew not where to keep it. So he put it on his head and there it remained. A year later he was given another piece and he put that on his head over the old piece. It is madness to bring such things under intellectual analysis. Feeling alone understands and worships such sublimity of feeling. Personal love given to the Guru is our discipleship. But we have no right to call others to discipleship unless the Guru is revealed in us and the soul of man is instinctively attracted to that Great Love. To other men the call will come direct. We have got a bad habit from the modern Christian missionary of going with the Bible in hand in the dust and noise of the streets, saying "*Believe in Jesus or you are for ever damned.*" None has the right to preach such things which are on the face of it, concerned with personality. Is it not shameful that we go and auction our Beloved for the fun of preaching a sermon that has but one effect of causing hatred between man and man? Because of my personal love of my Beloved, I should be so radiant that my radiance should conceal me and my Beloved from all. And yet my radiance should be a revelation of Him, as is the fragrance of the rose. It is certainly a tiresome futility for us to go impressing on the busy world of to-day that unless they keep long hair and wear turbans they cannot understand the Guru. The Guru is already diffusing his mind in the world-mind and if, like other theologians and priests, we strive to force upon the world our particular theology and rites and symbols we shall certainly fail. As the shape of nose and ear and eye cannot be limitations for the ecstasy of the soul, so no symbol, no rite, no particular form, no particular virtue or vice can impede the inner realization of the great ideals of the Guru But as the mystic expressional types of the Guru's mind, we have to roam in this world and spread the fragrance of the Guru with the braid-knot he gave us, and the flowing beards. Our shapes indeed can, in no sense, be considered symbols. But more important is the expression of the Sikh soul through their medium, and if that expression is lacking, our very life and body, whether our head be dressed or clean shaven, are meaningless superstitions. To a person given to religion, as one given to intense human love, trifles relating to the soul are more essential than the realms of silver and gold. Surely for such people the very superstitions contain more reflections of truth than the gathered facts of the learned people of the world. If one who is at peace and fully intoxicated on those delectable heights closes his eyes in ecstasy, this closing of his eyes is no symbol of religion and yet, in a sense, it is. So should be with us Sikhs, the wearing of His knot, His beard, His shape and His obedience. Our form and shape of the Guru will radiate with His Inspired and extraordinary humanity. Lacking that one thing, all shall be lacking. Without that spirit within us both life and death are devoid of meaning and truth.

XI

NOTES ON ART AND PERSONALITY
FROM THE SIKH VIEWPOINT

First, life. Then, its expression. The plum and the peach, if they are alive, must burst into a white universe of flowers when spring comes. Out of every bud a stream of flowers flows and engulfs them entire. The living peach and plum are thus at that moment unconscious of any outer universe but of their own flowers. This spontaneous expression of the mystery of life, at once so metaphorical and symbolical, gives us a way to approach art. All art activity is silent and intense in the depths of being. The moments of its expression are like the visits of angels few and far between, but its labour at the roots is continuous. And something happens, may be after centuries, after aeons, when all of a sudden, it bursts out into a rain of flowers. What is spring to trees, is inspiration to human race. And it is worth while to put up with a thousand winters for the sake of one day of blossoming as in spring. The highest and most perfect individual is he who brings this spring of inspiration to man. Being anything or any person below this perfection is of no abiding interest to art and the artist. Touched by His breath, the dead and the dying, the mean and the wretched, the sinful and the poor, spring into rage and become perfect and beautiful in a moment. This strange but oft repeated cosmic phenomenon of Nature is generally forgotten by us. The best literature, the best art, the most creative art-impulse of any race, at any time of human history, as to-day always rained and rains from Heaven on man, Greatness flows to him. And the creations of that wondrous period of his inspiration become the noble classics of the human race, in all aspects of its social life. Music, dancing, poetry, painting, sculpture, came out from happy and freed hearts, as the golden oranges bend with their profusion the delicate boughs of the orange tree. The golden harvests then ripen in such abundance that for centuries man reaps them and they still stand there waving in their original glory. For ever, a dream beautiful. This dream lasts for ever. The ideals pervade life. And life grows. There can be no democracy in the soul of Art. 'Democratic Art' is like the growth of grass in the meadows with a few tiny blue bells dancing. It may be pretty, but just pretty and nothing more. Art must agitate our souls. It must churn the blue ocean and, out of it bring a new sun and a new moon for the human race. Anything short of a cosmic upheaval of the soul-consciousness of man as a whole race, its uplift as a whole race even to a few inches higher from where it was, is imitation, not genuine art. Imitation has its uses in schools as forms of training but that constitutes no grand expression of the Divine Inspiration. Slaves alone appreciate microscopic drops on the lotus leaves, the freed men play with the sea and the sun and the moon. Till Beethoven gave his symphonies, all thought their music was perfect. One freed genius freed human thought to a new infinite perspective of the art of music. But Beethoven brought it out of his own soul. Beethoven starts a new epoch in himself. I do not think kingship of any kind is greater than this absolute despotism of an inspired man who opens a new subjective universe before us. Now, painters painting Beethoven's symphonies in colour is criticism of art, not art. The bold and astonishing originality, as I have said, man-transmuting originality, is the first sign of the true artist. Mr. Okakura is rightly bitter against imitation when he says, "Imitation whether of Nature, of the old masters, or above all of self, is suicidal to the realization of the individuality, which rejoices always to play an original part, be it of tragedy or comedy in the grand drama of life, of man and of Nature."

Rich kingship of soul flowers. The artistic consciousness is free, freedom follows. And in a great sense it is true that nothing can make man free but art.

I quote Okakura again when he says so beautifully, "Fragments of nature in her decorative aspects, clouds black with sleeping thunder, the mighty silence of pine forests, the immovable serenity of the snow, the ethereal purity of the lotus rising out of darkened waters, the breath of starlike plum flowers, the stains of heroic blood on the robes of maidenhood, the tears that may be shed in his old age by the hero, the mingled terror and pathos of war, and the waning light of some great splendour—such are the moods and symbols into which the artistic consciousness sinks before it touches with revealing hands that mask under which the universe hides. Art thus becomes the moment's repose of religion, or the instant when love stops half unconscious on her pilgrimage in search of the Infinite, lingering to gaze on the accomplished past and dimly seen future—a dream of suggestion, nothing more fixed—but a suggestion of the spirit, nothing less noble." With this ideal of Art before you, you can now pass before your imagination's eye, the glorious pageant of the Asiatic life that was inspired by the yellow-robed perfected humanity of Lord Buddha. The Buddhistic Art, that blossomed like the flower-floods of that Asiatic spring, is the symbolic and metaphoric expression of the inner sovereignty that was experienced by the poor and the rich alike. The Lotus Throne of Buddha, in fact, became the lotus throne for everyone. If it was democracy of men, each seated on his throne. Lord Buddha was not one of this democracy of the Spring. He was the hidden secret of the Breath of Spring, which made the blossoming of all with that miraculous suddenness possible. To Buddha raised every flower his crown and song in utter thankfulness and all submitted absolutely and unconditionally in joy of the Pure. And sister Nivedita thus sums up in her beautiful words the atmosphere that the, Buddha created by his personality. "To him (Okakura), it is not the ornamental or industrial features of his country's art which really form its characteristic elements, but that great life of the ideal by which it is hardly known as yet in Europe. Not a few drawings of plum blossoms but the mighty conception of the Dragon, not birds and flowers but the worship of Death, not a trifling realism however beautiful but a grand interpretation of the grandest theme within the reach of human mind, the longing and desire of Buddha-hood to save others and not itself—these are the true burdens of the Japanese Art."

So we see how birth of the Buddha in India agitated the soul of Asia. The life of the Asiatic races of China and Japan was inspired by the Buddha. So true Artistic expression of the soul-consciousness of a people is not so much in the nature of an *acquired achievement* as the spontaneous outflow of a spiritually rich self-realization.

The Gurus have altered our ideals of inner self-realization. "Know Thyself", is only partially right. The true artistic consciousness or religious consciousness blossoms in its own inner beauty when the inner self of man and the outer self of nature unite. Both partake of Reality which is beyond both. This union is rare and is not an individualistic but a cosmic phenomenon of life. Those who sat in caves, and meditated and found God in their soul, the so-called *Yogin* idealist, the *Zens* of Japan, were not truly spiritual; they were still intellectual, the abstractionists, poor moralists who set themselves, in pride of intellectual abstraction, as gods. On the other hand, those who rejected the subjective realities and sought Truth only in the outer objects and their beauty as realized by the senses, the so-called Realists, also were intellectual Their art too, wholly intellectual, touches in its rare flights the spiritual. There is thus no difference between the Greek ideals of old and the Art-ideals of the East *which are based on metaphysics*. The Greek sculptor rejects human flesh and endeavours to realize his ideal man in Apollo through the imagined pure medium of marble, it is as intellectual a representation of reality as of those who carved the images of the ecstasy of Lord Buddha in the large statues of stone. In fact when artistic consciousness wishes to express itself that way, it assumes the intellectual expression only. It can get to no other, because, after all, it is the intellectual sympathy that the artistic expression wishes to create. Hence it is that the Gurus do not consider *artistic expression* which needs must be intellectual. They insist first on artistic life and most on artistic inside, on the flame of inspiration burning within at the centre. The rest must follow. According to the Is, the spiritual expression of personality can only come through feeling born and bred in the human flesh. Human flesh is the imperfect medium through which the Gurus wish to express the Perfect. Beauty is neither outside, within the reach of the realist, nor inside, within the reach of the idealist, as both are seeking an intellectual abstraction. It is beyond intellectual abstractions, in the actual subjective spiritual union of the spirit of man with that of the universe or Nature. This union takes place rarely as a cosmic phenomenon. And the whole life waits for its happening. And as planets revolve without haste, without rest, so we men have to go on waiting for that great spiritual fulfilment through all our pursuits of pain and pleasure, of vice and virtue, of intellectual realization and of emotional expressions of extraordinary moods of ourselves, till we meet Him—the Artist. Our True Spiritual Religion and Art start after meeting Him, for He is so beautiful that however we may will otherwise we cannot thenceforward forget Him. Near Him or away from Him, we live in aching remembrance of Him. This aching remembrance is our religion, we cannot but be religious after seeing Him. We are driven to be religious. Aching remembrance is spontaneous in the inspired ones when they are away from him. The moments of union are rare and so love, according to the Gurus, is but aching remembrance. It is very unlucky that, according to the Gurus, there can be no religion and no art for you till you have met Him. So, all the Gurus condemn ceremonial, theological routines. It is better to freshen the soil with a few furrows, than to go to a temple to pass through a routine which has no meaning for an unawakened soul. As the expression of the life of disciples can only be spiritual; so the art of the Guru is creation of the Divine Personality out of the Human Substance.

Human flesh that is radiant with life, vital, vitalising nectarian, immaculate, beautiful is the only medium for the artists of aching remembrance. And the chief aim is to make the human flesh worthy enough for enclaying God in it, all else is mere means.

I start all kinds of arts. From my eye, let Leonardo da Vinci remember the eyes of Christ. From my tresses let them remember the braids of Jesus. I not only ache with remembrance, but I produce the same aching pain in others. I am, as the Guru says, the legion. I refuse to be only one flower like the Brahman intellectual. I aspire to be the spring. My own salvation is not what I desire. Let all be saved. "Save them through whichever door of mercy thou mayst choose, O Lord!"

"My disciple is he who aches with love and makes others ache with love."

O Sikh youth of the Punjab! I hang my head in shame when I see you buying and selling ugly, obese, flesh-coloured smudges of ink blue and red and yellow, with no eyes, no head, no hands and feet, as the portraits of your Gurus who bestowed Buddhahood on many of their disciples. You read this in your history. No one ever, in the first 500 years or more after the Buddha, painted or sculptured Him. They only had a ladder with steps of the Buddha painted or sculptured on the rungs. This was all the portrait they made of their God. For five hundred years or more of *Dhyani* worship, they lived in silence about it, till they saw the Buddha in *Dhyanum* and with that divine aching remembrance becoming ecstatic they met Him. And now, however intellectual a phenomenon, how soothing it is to the soul to look at the ecstatic bliss of *Dhyani Buddha;* the appreciation of the *Dhyani* creations is fugitive.

When I stand before the pictures you call those of the Gurus, I feel as much disgusted as when I look at the ugly idols of Krishna of the Hindus in the temples of Vrindavan. You will be killed by this mean imitation of others' passion. Because Christians have been lucky to illustrate the Bible by the paintings of Italian masters, you must also imitate them to make your religion popular. Woe unto that religious preaching which needs the support of such soul-less imitations. For goodness' sake, burn all your canvases and throw your brushes away. You are not yet risen to the level of men and the craft of the artist is far above your reach. You are not yet able to grasp the essentials even of the intellectual appreciation of the Art of the Beautiful. You need yet learn how to wear a pearl necklace and how to adorn yourself. You must needs be decorated and beautiful to go and dare approach the Beautiful.

I have always thought that as there has risen no new Chaitanya in Bengal, the Bengal school of art is only a farce, an imitation. I feel spiritually happy when I look at the reproductions of the Ajanta cave frescoes, but I am disgusted with seeing the obliqueness of the paintings of the Bengal School, which is merely a mental concept. The imitation of such a specialised and delicate, almost spiritual, technique as of the Ajanta devotees, so apparent in the Bengal School, is sickening.

From the kind of pictures, however, you the Sikhs of the Punjab love, I feel that your soul of art is dead. You fail to show even the instincts of a spiritual aspirant. Pray, be silent, till life gathers in you and bursts out of itself. Till then it is better to cry than to go on rhyming 'him' with 'dim' and call it poetry of any kind. It is better to weep silent tears of prayer than to sing your hymns with the bass sound of the leathern harmonium. It is far more artistic to have a clean house, with pure, snow-white, lime-washed walls or even mud-washed as of the *Janglis* of the Punjab *bars*, than to hang up the headless Baba Deep Singh Shahid, as you say, with so much unregenerate flesh lumps with that label. Sickening! And you all stand and stare at your walls saying, "what a martyr!"

Let me tell you frankly, your outlook is much too dirty, dusty, weary, busy-bodied, to be anything near the sources of the creation of artistic forms or literature of any kind. All your monthlies are only fit for the dung-heap. Most of us calling ourselves literary lions are but dust-bins in which gathers the dirt of the worldly-wise. People who are spiritually or artistically rich in any way preserve themselves. They shudder at the idea of self-spending in worldly pursuits. They prefer death by starvation to living by deceiving people on a smaller or larger scale.

The philosopher seeks purity in the mineral, more than in the animal kingdom, little knowing, that perhaps what he calls sin in man is more precious a virtue than the dead glitter of gold. Of course, all organic things rot; man too, woman too. But rotting itself shows more life, when I see the oxen eating and eating straw, I look at them for long, since this act of gluttony, when they have such large bodies, is the highest spiritual act, compared with the non-eating of a huge boulder. Senses and their excitements and pleasures too, of animals, including the human animal, are, from this viewpoint, highly interesting spiritual acts. I think the bullock is a saint when eating and the cow when licking her calf. When one prefers the beauty of a snow peak to that of the white brow of a maiden, he shows inferior spiritual taste. Life interests the artist, and not the dead conceptions of it, however grand and sublime they may be, so to say, to look at. The face of the man, more than the sparkle of the diamond. To the artist, the goat that eats grass, gives birth to a kid, and suckles him, is more spiritual a phenomenon than the sunset or the sunrise or a hundred fleeting colours of the sky; the latter are no use, except to choose from, for the colours on his brush to paint a goat. For him nature is diffused, dim personalities in the making and man the spiritualised, sublimated image of it. And he flies, seeking the purity of the union of soul, both to man and to nature. His feelings are personal. And his art converts the universe into the deity of the temple of his heart. Well does Victor Hugo say, "Reduction of the whole universe to a single being and expansion of that single being to God is love." Diamonds and rubies, pearls and gems, art-creations in marble and in colours, the flower and the fruit, are in the hands of artists just a beautiful alphabet which has its full meaning only when it spells the name of the Beloved, This is the great spiritual motif of the Guru's Ideal of Art.

The Guru contemplates on feeling. "Feeling is all in all". Man in conceived as feeling in flesh, as divine act in flesh, as God's word in flesh. And while feeling creates its own new forms, imitation cannot. Imitation is like making dead statues of marble. It is of no interest to the artist of the Guru. Imitation is repetition that has no meaning. The way Potiphar's wife falls in love with Joseph is beyond all repetition.

The Buddha coming between the doe and the hunter, is the final form of that feeling. Jesus saying to Mary "Go, woman, and sin no more," and puffing the Pharisees to shame shall for ever remain above all following.

Mohammed's weeping like a man on the grave of his slave, Sayid, is unique. Omar's way of treating his slaves on an equal footing with himself is beyond all imitation. No one after them in the Moslem world can be capable, in that way, of divine democratic feeling.

Guru Nanak is glad to see feelings being sculptured like this in human history. But he is sick of men who wish to imitate and follow, and be but dead quotations of great things. To the Guru, the human history is the history of such feelings, the rest is of no consequence at all.

It is not quite true that beauty is all within me. Beauty is equally all outside me. But what is true is this, that it is vain to fly after the beauty outside me to possess it. I must receive the supersensation of beauty and absorb it into my blood. One who breathes beauty is an artist, according to the Guru. Man should be the most effective shock-absorber of the self-sensations of beauty. The Guru says, "Eat thrills, absorb joy and be more beautiful than all outside beauty." Man perfected by devouring the lightning flashes of the whole cosmos scintillating with beauty, is invoked by Guru Nanak. His ideal artist is Christ, Buddha, and not the one who makes images of them in colour or stone. The latter is the representative appreciation of this spiritual artist as if by the people. It is the intellectual critic that expresses himself in marble or in colour; all so-called art below that is but purer form of mere criticism. The so-called art is the excitant of higher moods in which one is made capable of true appreciation.

Guru Nanak says, the truest self-restraint that transmutes corruptible flesh into immaculate flesh is born of glorious rapture of the Beautiful in nature and in man. Thus *Simrin* is more artistic than the so-called 'ethical.' Once the human flesh is made immaculate by *Simrins*, Guru Gobind Singh calls it '*Kanchan si* Kaya'– flesh as immaculate as gold. It is worshipful. It is the highest and the noblest art creation. From that standpoint, where flesh by the solution of God's music in it has been transmuted, the Guru condemns both the contrition of saints at the sight of human flesh and their self-abandonment and flesh-mortification and their getting to God through penances; and he also condemns all the pleasures which result in self-putrefaction of human flesh. Hence His ideal of spontaneous self-restrains, effortless effort to chisel one's flesh into the immaculate beauty of the divine. Such spontaneity of the life beautiful and magnetic, is freedom. According to these standards of the Guru, the flesh is made evanescent on the artistic creation of a perfected man, the Temple of God.

Nothing dies. The voice that I have heard, I shall hear again. The eyes that have looked alive once, shall gaze into my eyes again. That intense imagination which can bring before the vision's eyes the face of the Beloved, as the regions of hell and heaven rolled before Dante's eyes, it is intense imagination which is the essential quality of art. And such imagination is not speculative at all, it is the artistic carver of the myriad images of the Beloved.

To get rid of the nausea of visible physical putrefaction of human flesh that is the result of sensual pleasure as sought by the Romans and to get a cure for the sickness of the intellectual putrefaction in mental moralities, as sought for by the Aryan and Non-Aryan priests, it is certainly soothing to look at an ideal woman shaped in marble, almost made a goddess by the Greek sculptors. The woman in the street disgusted the intellect and the woman thus sculptured out of the imagination of the artist recreated the divine worship. It must needs be offered to the real woman. The meanest flower gains unsurpassable beauty when touched by this feeling of worship. A green leaf, touched by Mary Magdalene for her offering to Christ, becomes invaluable. All great art must be similar revelation of feeling, deep and mute and alive, as lightning asleep in the cloud. Then, it may lift a leaf or a flower or cast just a glance; it is the incessant creator of the Beautiful that it has seen.

Just as metaphysics was an intellectual attempt to soothe the ruffled intellect, so were the arts of sculpture and painting, the intellectual attempts of human genius to soothe the disgusted feeling. And a well-carved image of even a prostitute in marble soothes us, while the vileness of ,a prostitute in life may irritate us. Seeing the painting of a lovely woman, we may fall in love with her for a whole lifetime though if she be found in life it may be difficult to live with her for a day. Art, thus, is contemplation of the Beautiful by the artist as an unattached witness. This contemplation lifts us above ourselves, above body and mind, and elevate our consciousness; it beautifies our vision. Through art, we see beauty everywhere. A rain of beauty seems to drizzle. Everything grows beautiful. In this bliss of *Nirvana,* the body is not remembered by the buddha; his peace overflows and engulfs it entire. Now, an artist, who has to give us an image in stone of that self-realization, has to ignore the physical. It is wonderful that *Dai Butsa* of Kama Kura sends a thrill of a living awe of the great person of Lord Buddha, and one never knows that He had a body like us. I stood entranced before *Dai Butsa* at Kama Kura, and I only contemplated and contemplated with dosed eyes all open and with open eyes all closed and I saw nothing, and felt nothing physical but only inner peace. Only holiness. Only a strange life shining in the crest jewel that the Buddha's great statue bore, on the glorious knot of his Nepal tresses. Surely both artistic contemplation as in art forms and metaphysical contemplation of man and nature as in mental abstractions are essentially intellectual appreciations only of the Divine that the Buddha realized. The Guru says, if one has that artistic attitude continuously with one, looking at all living things and dealing with all living things in that spiritual sense, then the true art becomes manifest. And who is the greater artist, one who looks at many living things and vibrates in sympathy with them, or one who, to start with, renounces them and then writes poems comparing the quivering of the petals of a rose to the trembling of the petaline lips of a bride that is waiting for her bridegroom? The Hindu *Brahman* seeker renounced his wife and children and sought their likeness in imagined gods, and in suns and stars and trees and rivers and birds, for, in spite of him, they all went with him wherever he went. And the Greek artist renounced his gods in flesh only to find them in marble. Renunciation in both cases was a meaningless vanity; neither got the peace of formlessness, for the one had a form and a frame himself and he could not jump out of his skin, and the other had not the peace of loneliness to contemplate perfection in marble, for, his creations still smiled even in death.

The Guru says, human flesh rots without 'Naming Him.' The state of spiritual immortality is of perpetual youth when man becomes a lyric of love. When one reaches the spiritual depths of the soul and lives attuned to that wondrous richness of the ecstatic life, no misery of whatsoever kind, no suffering how acute, no sorrows how gnawing, can dim the lustre of the smile of that great deep, musical life. It indicates poverty of the spiritual inner life, when the ideals of art or religion seem to incline towards the purity of the marble or the spotlessness of light, except as an intellectual excitement to the realization of the spiritual beauty of the flesh. The black stains of sin on the white apparel of the sinner have more of perfection, if the sinner be made more beautiful of soul thereby. The one diamond shines amidst numerous particles of sand. Saint Francis kisses the leper's wounds, while a man, poor of soul, flies from the sickness to save his life from infection. The other day, when the influenza, epidemic raged, men and women were dying like flies, and some of my dearest friends were lying down with it and no one to look after them. I was down with the physical infirmity. I only wept. My tears called to the unknown St. Francis of the Sikh Punjab. "Puran, I will go and look after your friends!" Apparelled in a white silk gown, an old man beaming with the youthful joy of a new bridegroom of eighteen, goes. He goes and beats with his stick the influenza out of the bed of my dear ones. He sits with them, lies with them, the inner magnet of his attracts the disease out of them to himself and in himself burns a conflagration in which all bacilli die. Immaculate, he comes out and he saves a few lives. Unless this great flame burns within, a mere fatalist is stupid, for he idly courts death. The real victor defeats death and foils the 'foes of the life-spark.' Jesus heals the leper, St. Francis kisses him. There is difference in the inner potential. When one is rich within, of soul, of spiritual life, when one is the veritable King of Glory, one does not despise frail mortal forms to which life clings so tenaciously. The Buddha accepts the invitation of a courtesan, while lovers of God and soul that imagine such realities in an impersonal light fly from such 'moral filths.' He was attracted by the perfection of life that trembled on the lips of the courtesan, the lips that invited him. These distinctions of virtue and vice are unreal to the poet's mind, who is looking at deeper levels of life where there is perennial beauty, music and love. The surface veils part like clouds that are torn asunder with such splendour by the rising sun, and the eye, enamoured of life's mystery is red with wonder that sees but can never voice it forth!

XII

'GURU PRASAD'—BY HIS FAVOUR

In *Japuji* of Guru Nanak, there is a phrase that refers to a cosmic phenomenon that takes place when the disciple gets embedded in his soul-consciousness——nucleus of the life of the spirit, small as a mustard grain, bright as a point of fire. Thenceforward the disciple lives inspired of it, and is sustained by it as the mother is by the child, the artist by beauty, the opium-eater by his dose, the Majnun of his Leili. The disciple dies when this spark of life is extinguished. The disciple is in aching struggle to keep this flame burning in his soul day and night. His body thenceforward is a temple, his life a wholly dedicated life-in-memorium. His lungs breathe the moral spirit of the spiritual universe, and his eyes see what those around him do not see. His attitude undergoes a revolutionary transformation. This is true of those who are truly *converted*. The man unconverted sees the world as a solid reality; the man converted sees there are greater realities than these and before those these facts of this world are mere fictions, illusions. Great is his sorrow and he feels comforted when living by the side of this inner fire. Nothing else is of equal interest to him. The disciple, thus, is of the sublimated humanity, his dwelling place is not our earth.

Foolish is all talk and action of converting any people to this faith or that, to this religion or that, for the truly converted man becomes a veritable angel and transcends all miserable imitations of the crawling insects that make bacterial colonies on a piece of bread or jelly here and there and call themselves Hindus, Christians, Sikhs, Moslems, Buddhists and Zorastrians. When a man is converted, the cocoon of illusion breaks and the butterfly of the soul wings away into the Infinite rapture of the blue that has no definition of any kind. True freedom is there, nowhere here.

This significant phrase is *Guru-Prasad*. Guru Nanak says, "O disciple, your life of the spirit begins when the rain of His Mercy falls on you. It is the favour of the Guru that starts your soul on its journey. You commence with his benediction and blessing." This favour makes manifest to you, your personal God Who thenceforward lives in your soul and works to free you into the freedom of love. All religions of man are stupors without this cosmic phenomenon taking place in the soul-consciousness of man. No spiritual regeneration is possible for one without conversion. Foolish is the sacred thread. Foolish is circumcision, Foolish is worship in temples and churches and mosques. Without this spark of life come from Heaven and without its being embedded in one's consciousness, it is all sorrow, misery, distress, death. And with it glowing within man's soul, it is all joy, prosperity, and freedom and immortality. The tongue of this spark licks the individuality into a divine shape. It is the maker of Divine Personality. Bhai Gurdas, the Sikh apostle, says, "Naming Him is licking the very slab of stone in to the image of God."

The spiritual history of man is the continuous story of such conversion through the phenomenon of *Guru Prasad*, His favour.

It is a phenomenon in the moral world, as cosmic as the revolution of the solar system. The Guru-personality is impersonal but when it reacts on an individual, it becomes personal God and the consequent inspiration and companionship of His presence becomes continuous. This is the great technical difference between the Brahmanical Man-worship as Guru-worship and Guru Nanak's ideal of Guru. Guru Nanak always takes care to say, the true Guru, Sat-Guru, that is his ideal of the Guru-consciousness. It enters into man's life as the love of a woman enters into the married life of man. All are women, women are impersonal, but the woman becomes personal.

In the system of Guru Nanak, the word *Guru* is used in the sense of nature, the Cosmic Personality impersonal. And the favour of that Personality is the symbolic expression in poor language of man of the great moral phenomenon that brings about the true conversion of man to the life of the spirit when he renounces without renouncing the shadow of himself and faces the sun by mere orientation of the direction of his soul. Guru Nanak asks man to wait in an infinitely passive mood for the reception of this little grain and to wait, for ever toiling for it, as the mother of pearl waits for it and then closes to fashion a pearl around it. The man then becomes as a pearl in his angelic purity and his very flesh becomes immaculate by the influx of the Divine Spirit. This infinitely passive mood is spoken of by Guru Nanak as being as restlessly active as the attitude of the bride waiting for the bridegroom. Poor words convey the meaning but partially. The bride is passive and active at once. Guru Nanak conveys thus by contradictory terms a suggestion of the life that is to be lived and not merely talked about.

Guru Nanak teaches the surrender of self and yet puts a sword in the hands of his disciple to be a free man. They of the old musty non-violent Brahmanical ideals of the mineral kind of peace and purity fail to understand Guru Nanak when he rides a white steed as Guru Gobind Singh and a thousand swords rain their flashes.

The very immensity of the life of the spirit makes all our descriptions and definitions miserable. And it is the life of the spirit that must contradict itself in infinite directions and on planes of thought and action to be alive. Only some petrified statues of particular poses of spirituality can be comprehended by one particular set of mental concepts about reality and truth. The inspired life in its living moments must for ever baffle our sensual definitions and views and viewpoints of it.

Guru Gobind Singh is Guru Nanak at the climax of his spiritual glory. And those who have drunk deep of the spirit of Buddhism as engrafted on the race of Yamoto in Japan can appreciate the loftiness of the spiritual life which is in the holy shadow of Guru Gobind Singh on horse-back.

There are many illustrious occasions in history when this spiritual phenomenon of Guru-consciousness entering into the disciple-consciousness has cleaned the personality of the disciple from within and made of him a veritable God. Mary Magdalene was thus healed. To me, no other, healing of Christ is so miraculous as the healing of Mary. The greatest miracle that a man of *Simrin* performs is to heal the wounded soul, wounded by sin or by grief, or by distress or by life which to serious minds is the greatest suffering of all. And then to seed it with the shining grain of faith, a very little grain that by its inner radiance so blesses the disciple that in utter thankfulness the disciple falls on his knees, closes his eyes and says, "Mercy, Mercy, Mercy!"

In fiction, the Bishop of D—, in *Les Miserables* so blesses Jean Valjean and orientates the direction of his soul. This one act depicted by Victor Hugo makes me think that Hugo understood the Christianity of Christ better than Tolstoy of Russia. The conversion of Sayid Khan, the Mughal general, besieging the fort of Anandpur took place in the remarkable setting of a pitched battle. Sayid Khan, like the Hindu intellectuals and the non-violents of to-day and all curious sentimentalists of all times, people who make of spirituality a day toy of their own mind, doubting how Guru Gobind Singh could be as spiritual as Guru Nanak. And he was still doubting when along comes Guru Gobind Singh riding direct towards him on His purple steed. And Sayid Khan points his rifle at the Guru, but the bullet misses. And Guru Gobind Singh addresses him thus, "Come, Sayid Khan, what are the doubts you have?"

"Teach me about Thyself," replied Sayid Khan.

"If that is the game and nor war, thei put your head on my stirrups," said the Guru.

Sayid Khan alighted from his horse and as he lay at the feet of Guru Gobind Singh, the Soldier-Guru touched him with the sharp edge of his spear. That touch was enough. Sayid Khan was converted. And Sayid Khan went towards the Himalayas renouncing all to cultivate the spiritual art of the Guru's *Simrin*. And thousands were so touched by the Guru's arrow 'and made *Arahata*. Guru Gobind Singh made not only men but high spiritual geniuses. He was in love's high ecstasy, when on horseback.

The spirit of the Sikh that flashes now and then in the Punjab is the remnant fire of the Guru's bosom.

XIII

THE BROTHERS OF THE TRESS-KNOT OF GURU GOBIND SINGH

This Brotherhood was inaugurated by Guru Gobind Singh. It is the Brotherhood of Knights of Honour who live the inward life of *Nam* and *Simrin*. They are those whose presence sheds the Nectar of Peace all round. They desire neither crowns here nor paradise hereafter, only that they may deserve His Love, His Mercy. They desire neither the mystic joys of *Yoga*, nor the sensual pleasures of *Bhoga*, only that they may be filled with the Nectar of His Love, their little chalices of heart fill with the dew of His Psalms. They are full of the philosophic sorrow of life and they cry and fly as rain, birds to catch the auspicious drop of Heaven with which to quench their thirst and the thirst of all those who suffer. It is by repetition of the Beloved's name that they can maintain their spiritual state and as their thirst for it is infinite, their repetition like, the songs of birds is incessant. The secret of spiritual manhood is the inspired love for the Beloved and this love consists in the perpetual singing of the Guru's Psalms and the Guru's Name.

The inspired personality of this Brotherhood is song-strung, love-strung, strong and gentle, fearless, death-despising, even death-courting, seeking no rewards for incessant self-sacrifice in the name of the Master, dying like moths round the lamp, living like heroes, shining like orbs intoxicated, sweetly exhilarated every moment of life, elevated above the sorry details of things, wishing well to the whole universe of life, and desiring nothing but lyrical repetition of His Name.

The Name, breath by breath is the Truth, the personal Truth and the whole Truth for the Brothers of the Tress-Knot of Guru Gobind Singh.

As the Guru says, the *modus operandi* of realizing such a dynamic personality, all so impersonal like one of God, is by keeping burning for ever the lamp of *Nam*, the Light of Life, in the shrine of one's heart. "He who has the light burning for twenty-four hours in the shrine of the heart is the pure *Khalsa*."

The symbolic representation of that light is the repetition of the Name. The breath of man is to resound with it, his pores to flow with its nectarian bliss. The eyes go themselves half-upward under the upper lids, the forehead seems to be filled with nectar as if it were a fountain and a thousand crystal streams flow down from this Himalaya, fertilising not one person, but all those who come under the influence of such a one. The personality of the Brother, being like a lake, a fountain, a river, emits spontaneous radiations of universal good-will, peace and love. It is all illumination around; no dark ghosts of evil can prowl near about such presences.

Their ethics are not of books, nor of algebraic formulae, nor of moral justifications cleverly patched up for certain so-called moral or immoral acts. They are in unison, by the impersonal nature of their holy unselfishness, with the soul of Nature. They are as the mountain, the river, the cloud, the flower. Wherever there is a rose, it must needs scent the surroundings. The Brother must fill the corner of the earth he is in, not only with the sweetness of his soul— it goes out of it in spite of him—but also with active sympathy. He is always the Prince of Compassion.

Guru Amar Das could not bear the weeping of a widow on the death of her husband, nor of a mother on the death of her son. And it so happened that the whole Goindwal, the

Master's residence, had no such sorrow during his lifetime. This is of the strange uniqueness of such genius. Guru Teg Bahadur could endure human suffering; his hymns are full of tears, of infinite renunciation, if thereby the miserable man could be made happy and free. Guru Gobind Singh's renunciation out of compassion for the miserable slaves of India is infinite. He sacrifices even his God for the amelioration of the condition of the miserable.

Consistent with the inspiration of the lives of his spiritual ancestry of the Ten Gurus and their disciples, his forefathers, the Brother is he who carries the torch of inspiration burning, not in pursuance of any, vows, not for the sake of any gain, but as so ordains the Order of Guru Gobind Singh and so constrains without constraining and so restrains without restraining, his love, his *Nam* and *Simrin*. The Brother is the vehicle of His Spirit. As the lamps of *Simrin* burn out, the Sikh dies. As the tree blossoms, so the Sikh blossoms with the joy of *Nam* and *Simrin*. As the tree offers its best to the roving winds, so the Sikh offers his all to all. For my ethical conduct, not I but He is responsible, who darts out shoots of trees in the spring, who makes the stars shine. I have learnt the secret of life and I let myself be but as a piece of cloud, raining when He bids me, and flashing lightning when He so bids. My acts are in consonance with my feelings—such is His pleasure. All events to me are also set in the same dreamy rhythm—such is His pleasure.

The truths of the world are falsehoods for me, their certainties to me are thoughts of darkness,—unreal, ghostly, apparitions of which I am afraid and from which I run away. My brotherhood is scattered in the history of man in rare persons. All those who call themselves Brothers but are not inwardly, spiritually, intentionally, intuitionally and subconsciously of the Guru, are struck off the roll. All those who attain the *Khalsa* state of the life of the spirit find entrance into the court of Guru Gobind Singh and they are of us. My Brotherhood is scattered in wind, water and fire and cloud and sun and star. I hear a greeting of this sacred secret Brotherhood from the petals of flowers, from the musical sculptured shapes of the beautiful aspects of natural scenery. The river is my brother and the wind my sister. The cloud sympathises with me. And the sun's love for me is limitless and unconditional. There is glory in the crowds of men and women, a rare gleam that is not seen in mere individuals, a flash that like out of the gathering of clouds comes out of the gathering of men. In all these are the gleams of the shining crest that the Master of this Brotherhood wears and rides past on His fairy purple steed by the door of the Brothers of the Faithful.

In the words of Bhai Vir Singh Ji, let me give the creed of this Brotherhood in five words, *"Nam, Dan, Snan, Kirt Karna* and *Wand Chhakna."*

- *NAM*—Naming Him, the secret of personality that has no personal aims, ambitions or selfishness.
Selfishness is transcended by love. So by living in Him, by Naming Him, by dying in Him. In love of Him, man attains his manhood, which is for ever divine and unselfish. The essential nature of the soul is unselfish. Realizing one's soul first through *Nam* constitutes the life of this Brotherhood. It is the maintenance of the spiritual attitude by physical effort while in this physical universe of incessant struggle.
- *DAN*—Giving. Giving away all one has, in spontaneous sympathy, in infinite philosophic sorrow for the living and in infinite but silent, unaggressive, unobtrusive, spontaneous zeal for doing good to the living, as does the rose of the river. It is an attitude of the elevated life that gives without knowing. As hotter objects impart heat to the colder objects around by the difference in potential, so does a Brother of the Tress-knot of Guru Gobind Singh give. *Dan,*

certainly, does not mean in the Guru's Brotherhood, the conscious contributions of charity, a giving of alms. "All belong to the Guru;" so does the Brother feel, and always "All is His, nothing is mine." Such affectionate attitude never comes by any social codes or rules. It is nothing mechanical, it is deep and organic. This charity of the Brother flows like rivers out of his whole being. The Brother has foregone his self, his labour, his very flesh and blood, his life, and his soul, for the Beloved Master.

SNAN—Bathing the body with cold water; bathing the mind in the nectarian streams; bathing the soul in love of him.

KIRT KARWA—This is the symbolic phrase that knits Guru Gobind Singh's Brotherhood with the whole humanity of labourers. The Guru has no rich man, no idle rich man in his Brotherhood,—no place for him. All must labour, must sweat to create the foodstuffs, to create shapes out of iron, wood and stone, to work, to labour, and then to forego the fruits of labour. And in this spontaneous foregoing is the difference yet between the Brother and the modem labourer.

WAND CHHAKNA—Equal distribution of the fruits of labour. "Partake not of that bread which thou hast not split with thy Brother."

Guru Gobind Singh is the Guru of the modern times. He is a Prophet who has reconstructed human society in this Brotherhood of *Nam, Dan, Snan, Kirt Karna* and *Wand Chhakna*.

The Name, the Renunciation whole and entire, and the Bath in the infinite of body, mind and soul. On every member of humanity is laid the essential spiritual necessity to labour, and to create, and then not only to forego in any passive spirit the fruit of labour but to actively distribute its fruit equally amongst Brothers. If the Sikhs of the Punjab only faintly remind us of this Great White Brotherhood of Guru Gobind Singh, what matters it indeed, when the whole world is aspiring and suspiring from the underground towards it?

Here is an invitation from the Guru to the whole world; and who amongst us does not see the active but vague and subconscious response of the whole world to Guru Gobind Singh? His genius is to be understood by man after centuries when he has realized the Guru's spiritual Brotherhood.

Assuredly the slaves of India have not understood Him so far and are not capable of understanding His genius. The shadow of his large personality falls far away above the head of centuries and the so-called best intellectuals of India, when they spread out their mind to understand the Guru, get bruised by mere thorns and give Him up a something not as spiritual as Guru Nanak. All this indicates the darkness that surrounds them. If they cannot see Guru Gobind Singh as the highest, brightest culmination of Guru Nanak, assuredly they do not at all understand that King of Revolution of religious thought, the great Guru Nanak. In each of his mild words are concealed a myriad flames that split again and again like lightning into myriads of swords which writhe in human blood. The Name whose lyrical repetition is to found the future empire of the labouring man on *Love Labour* and *Utter Renunciation*.

The world of thought has yet to understand the Ten Gurus in splendour of their thought which has been misunderstood due to the Brahmanical language they had to employ to express themselves and to the Brahmanical environment which always has been inimical to the true cultural progress of man.

The genius of the Gurus' expresses their revolutionary thought by contradicting all that they say in that particular vernacular and leaving it to the reader to read the face of their idea made by the crossing of lines and planes of thought in context with their lives and deeds and the history they made, as the new and the nearest past for the Brotherhood of Love and Utter Renunciation they so created. It is my belief that, in one night and in one day, when the *Ideas* or the *Idea* of the Guru, which is a whole revolution in Eastern thought on religion and conduct of life, is seen and stated in its perfect simplicity and in a perfect language, the consciousness of the Ten Gurus will pervade the whole human culture and centuries of many-sided human progress may yet stand witness to the Glory of the Guru. I propose to discuss the revolutionary nature of these ideas at some other time. But let me say, that, assuredly, the Guru's religion is the religion of Nature and of the soul. It is absolutely different from the theological and philosophic nonsense of the Brahmans. It refuses to have any concern with the reality composed of a certain set of final mental concepts such as the Brahmanical philosophic speculations put forth. Concept are dead matter. The religion of the Guru is, briefly, the art of living, and keeping the divine light aflame, more artistic than metaphysical or theological, and more full of labour, craft, and the appreciations of the beautiful in man and nature and their handicraft. It is full of infinite joy and yet full of infinite sorrow. Joy in the Guru's system is the blossom of the tree of sorrow of life, Mere happiness of those who have not realized the sorrow of life is vanity, as frail and unsubstantial as the fading flush of the flowers that are plucked off their bush.

The Brothers of the Tress-Knot of Guru Gobind Singh are a *Sangha* in which woman take free and equal membership. For the first time in the history of the East, woman has been treated as equal to man. There is no such word as *Sikhni* in the Sikh literature made by the Guru. The Sikh, or the Disciple is a soul of sexless gender, it is the appellation given to all who join the *Sangha*. I am ashamed that the words *Sikhni* and *Singhni* have been introduced by the old social proclivities of the Hindu-born Sikhs.

The Buddha, at the persuation of his gentle and loveable disciple Ananda, inaugurated the order of nuns. And of the many disciples that gathered round Jesus Christ, some of the best were the women of Palestine. But here the Gurus reconstructed the society of the Servants of Love on equal rights of discipleship and love, both for man and woman. This Ideal of the Gurus is unique and revolutionary.

Come, then, ye, the Sikh youth of the Punjab, and hold aloft the Flag of the Guru, renouncing all in His Name! Let us be Brothers of the Tress-Knot of Guru Gobind Singh and refuse to belong to any mushroom growth of orders or societies or clubs of ha'penny tu'penny so-called prophets that are like weeds in this forest of life. The Brothers that have gone before us live on the other side of death. They come to us to aid us if we just turn our face towards them and desire aid. We are innumerable if we resign our souls and renounce the bodies, keeping them as mere vehicles, as that Great Brother of this *Sangha*, Christ, said of his body that it was but the vehicle of the 'Spirit of the Father.'

XIV

THE DOER OF GOOD AND
THE TOILER ON EARTH[1]

It was the City of the *Doer of Good*. He built mansions for the poor. The poor came in numbers. They had two meals a day, they had white clothes. But they remained poor. They quarrelled with each other. They stole each other's clothes. They fought and abused one another. And they had no peace. They still suffered; they wept and cried and felt miserable.

In the city where he dwelt, there were twenty thousand poor, but he could house in these mansions only about five hundred. And he thought he was doing good in providing food and clothes to so many of the poor unfortunates. He built schools to educate the poor. He gave free education. He gave books; writing materials, free board and lodging. Great was his reward when he saw a thousand young faces beaming like flowers in his school. And how they called him their father: And there was a glory round his acts of charity. But the educated graduates of his school still remained poor in thought and outlook. And he thought how good it was to educate so many poor children of his city!

Many were his deeds of charity, which his right hand did and his left hand knew not. And wherever he went, the people of the city looked up to him with admiration.

In the same city dwelt an unknown labourer. Let us name him *The Toiler on Earth*. He laboured and toiled and sweated for earning his bread. He was poor in the physical means of life, but rich in life itself. No one knew him. No one so poor as to notice him! For fifty years he dwelt in a mud-hut within the walls of the city of the *Doer of Good*, but he never thought there was any difference between him and the dove or the pigeon that flies so many miles a day to pick up a tiny grain. He never could think that there was any essential difference between him and the ox or the horse both of which toil and labour and sweat for the whole day to get just a meal. He sat looking at the horse, chewing the grass and comparing it with his act of chewing his bread and potato. And he felt the sorrow of life keenly. But he only lifted up his eyes, and a tear unseen by any eye rolled in them. At times it was lost, and sometimes it fell silently on his shirt.

One midnight, as the stars shone, he lifted up his eyes and prayed, "O God! How distressed is this world! There are hungry men, and naked children. There are bereft woman for whom no one cares. This vale is full of tears of misery. The empty laughter of many rich men sounds in my ears as cries, only shriller and more piteous than those of the widow and the orphan. People dying on the roadside for want of bread. Ants toiling for the rainy day and being crushed by the thousands under the footfall of an unwary traveller on the path of life. And I too poor to relieve this universal suffering." He had passed many such midnights. And he wept again and slept. That night there appeared to him an Angel in shining raiment, his face bright as the moon. The sweet soft light of his presence fell softly on his eyelids and the sleeper awoke.

"I am sent by the Master in response to Thy prayer O man! whose feeling for humanity is so keen. The Heavens have *seen* the misery. There we *see as* if a thousand swords stab thee and thou bleedest every day. And now for years."

"Mercy! Mercy! What are the commands of my Master?"

"Knowest thou not, O man, that doing good is an extremely difficult task and you have been desiring to do good?"

"Behold!" said the Angel and there appeared in that inner Heaven the radiant Divine Figure of the Prophet. And in the speech of silence, the Prophet showed him the marks of nails driven in his temples. And soon after, the Figure slowly disappeared.

"Have you seen, O Man! the nails driven in the temples of the Prophet?"

"Yes, but I have understood not what he said."

And the Angel explained, "He who raised the dead, healed the leper, saved the sinner, must suffer himself. It is by the quantitative exchange of the life-substance that such wonders can be done."

"But what can he do, who has no life substance?"

"No one has the life substance here on earth. The still, so to say, is here, but the *distillate of life,* the *quintessence* gathers in regions from where I come. From there flows the substance and lives in the hearts of rare geniuses on this earth."

"And how do men on this earth obtain it?"
"It is given unto those who are given the authority to heal the souls."
"And the bodies?"

"When souls are healed, the bodies follow." Christ when on earth awakened the soul. It is the *spiritually dead* who rise to life, to the reception of the Grace of Heavens. Raising of the dead bodies forms no part of Christ's life. Raising of the souls was his function, the bodies followed as follows the man his shadow."

"But who are given authority?"

"Only those who rise like trees upward to the pinnacle of sacrifice and surrender,—not of a dead mechanical kind, but a surrender, spontaneous and whole, which is the result of life lived in unison with the spirit of the great Cosmic Order of the Universe, briefly I call it, *Cosmic Surrender.* The *Cosmic Surrender* is not the end of knowledge, but the function of life, surrender that is not death, but the end of death. It is only then when man so self-realises life that he rises above all physical restraints and shines like a sun over the universe. And only those can relieve the suffering of men,—only those so blessed by Heaven. No one else."

And the *Toiler on Earth* was overwhelmed with grace. A magnetic stream of light, he saw, flowing unto him. And he felt as a woman feels when filled with the spirit of man. He became speechless with wonder. And the *authority* then passed on to him.

And the Angel continued "But, O man! you must remember what you call *suffering* is not the *suffering.* There are infinite aspects of suffering. There are infinite degrees of suffering. What you see in this world is just the beginning of it. Angels suffer, from infinite compassion,—that suffering is of the acutest. And the disembodied souls suffer more than the embodied."

As he said this, there appeared in the illumined firmament the emaciated naked figure of a woman. Her hair was dishevelled, her form utterly emaciated by sorrow. She had slender, beautiful arms and eyes burning, deep, liquid, velvety black. She was an ethereal figure of sorrow. And she went past the *Toiler on Earth* crying and bewailing. It was an exquisite beauty in distress.

"Have you seen her grief?" said the angel. "She died after having wasted the whole of herself in deep grief over the death of her husband. Her husband is in a quite different sphere. Behold!"

As the Angel lifted his hand, there the veil of the sky shook and through the rift peered a young man, an Adonis himself the peer of Apollo, laughing, smiling, with a rosary of shining emeralds. And his presence was brilliant like that of lightning. One could not gaze full at his beauty even with dreamy eyes in the dream.

"See how living he is. He is full of the life substance that can do good. And he frowns at times at the grief of his wife, but he cannot help her. Here personalities are notes of an exquisite music and only those in deep concord and in living assonance meet here."

"What about his wife? How long shall she cry in separation?"
"What will you say if I say for centuries."
"Terrible!"
"Is a hungry woman more miserable or she?"
"Love-pang is as the sword-stab. Mercy, Master, mercy!"
"Well, then. Suffering has its degrees. And one has to relieve suffering."

"I wish to relieve her suffering and make of her a musical note that may go and join her husband; who, too is waiting for her."

"But she is not in body. You are in body. You cannot relieve her."

"Who can relieve her?"
"Your Master."
"But I know my Master only through prayer."
"Yes, prayer when heard can relieve her."

"O Master! Pray relieve her suffering. How terrible it is to see a soul in agony. O Lord! It is unselfish agony. Her body is gone. Her soul is going."

A flash of lightning hovered over his head. His eyes closed, he was knocked down and lay almost dead. And the weeping spirit of the widow rose before his closed eyes and his enfeebled soul uttered very faintly "Mercy! Mercy!"

As he woke back, he saw the angel standing before him. The face of the *Toiler on Earth* was black with the soot of Sin, his left arm was paralysed and his heart full of misgivings.

"Have you seen the cosmic phenomenon, how the self-made sorrows of man are cut in the Heaven by the Almighty One?"

"Yes."
"Your face is black. Your left arm is paralysed. You are full of misgivings. Your beautiful faith is almost uprooted. Your soul is almost gone out of your body and is about to leave you. But the time is not yet come. Lo! I touch you to relieve your faith."

And the angel touched him and there returned to him the simple faith in renewed beauty and still more perfected simplicity.

"Mercy, Mercy!" he said with the new music of re-union with the Unseen.

"So a prayer has healed this disembodied *Virhani,* the spouse separated from her beloved. But do not think all prayers will be answered. You have not seen how great a war took place in a flash. Thousands of dark ghosts, her grief and suffering that assumed those horrible forms, stood by her like clouds gathered round a snow-peak and your prayer, as a matter of your preparation for some task yet to be given you, as an experimental test, was heard by your Master and at the signal from His brow, an over-whelming number of white angels gathered. And when dark spirits shook you and threw you down and had almost killed you by the very shock, the white angels swarmed and as the light destroys darkness, they destroyed the self-made records of sins of the woman who sinned for the love of him in deep ignorance. Sins are those thoughts that break our link with Him. Acts are never so sinful as the wrong inner thoughts. And behold!"

The angel lifted his hand, and there peered again that handsome angel with the rosary of emerald and by him stood, still more beautiful, his lover, the woman. Both were again together in the garden of smiles where raptures melted into raptures, where souls blended into souls, and music into music.

It was the birthday of the *Doer of Good,* and the whole city had turned out to do him honour. They were carrying him in a procession, driven in an eight-horsed carriage. A young couple that had come to the city of great fame to spend their days of honey-moon stood in a balcony watching the gaiety of the people and the grandeur of the procession. The young girl, a princess of beauty, a marvel of creation, stood by his side. Her dream-coloured beauty did set a new standard in every eye. And those who saw her, forgot their past experiences and started afresh a new life of admiration. Her face gave new consolation to the people, almost a new youth. She was beauty which had annihilated all flesh and comforted the faithless with spontaneous faith in the spirit of things. The misery of life was washed by a glimpse of her. She was a paradise of line and colour. She was a soul without a body that was feasting itself on the beauty of her young lover, a prince amongst men. And they both clung to each other doubting always if their separate bodies may not part them unawares from each other. They stood in the balcony clinging to each other so spiritually.

A great rush of men came. The procession halted just below them in the street. People swarmed up and down. The balcony gave way. The horses of the carriage of the *Doer of Good* took fright. The young stranger who fell was trampled down under their hooves. And the young girl who was caught by the spectators as she fell, unfortunately uninjured, cried frantically to be thrown down under the hooves of those death-horses, but no one listened to her. The procession parted on either side. The dead young man was lifted up and brought to her. She fell on his body crying to die, but she could not die. She was too young and full of life to die like that. She tore her breasts with her nails and bruised them. She tore her clothes threadbare and her finest bride's clothes were mere ribbons, both the shirt and the skirt mere hanging threads. Her veil cloth was gone. Bareheaded she bewailed hopelessly. Her long tresses, which he had kissed a hundred times a day, were let loose, full of dust and sorrow. Her eyes were swollen with weeping. Her distracted cries rent the sky. The whole procession cried round her and all wept in sympathy. And the *Doer of Good* came down from his carriage and stood by the bewailing nymph and could do nothing. He had millions still to build a separate mansion for this princess to pass the rest of her life in. But in the presence of that sublime, noble and majestic suffering, he was ashamed of his millions.

"Ah! What can my millions do for her? I am utterly helpless to assuage her pain," thought he, self-ashamed.

The young man was cremated, his bones and ashes taken away from her and thrown into the river. She was even more alone. Her tears had dried in a few days. But her eyes were full of pain that no one could bear. Sympathy poured in, in the form of dead gold, and palaces were thrown open to her. But the sight of palaces and offers of being made comfortable physically were as the cruel stabs of swords.

Under a tree of this city of fame came a great saint. They said he came from the Holy Tibet. An extraordinary man whom they call a typically *Yogin* and a *Brahmagyani*, a universally worshipped man. A picture of the Absolute, *'Nirwan-dwa-triguna-Atit'—unaffected by the opposites, as they say, and inured to the abstraction of the Absolute*. He smiled benignantly and spoke to no one.

They took this widowed princess to him. At sight of her, he was moved to speak to her.
"Daughter, this world is all perishable. Know this is the way and renounce your grief."
"I can renounce my grief, sir, if I can realize my beautiful one."
"It is the illusion of thine own senses. Renounce this also."
"Sir, I cannot. How can I renounce the life of my life?"

"But all this grief is mere vanity and pride. You are only weeping over your own happiness."

At these words, there was a tragic scene. She was tortured almost to death by this remark. She tore her clothes again as on the first day. She began tearing her limbs, hurting them and crying out:

"O people! for God's sake bring an axe and dismember me joint by joint. Starve me to death. Throw me before lions. Let my meat be the food of vultures. Oh! let me die, let me die."

The saint rose and stood by her and felt ashamed. He said to himself, "All this while I have been living in a fool's paradise, thinking I have achieved *Sidhi* (spiritual success of self). This grief is a greater and nobler achievement than my dead *samata—sameness under all conditions*. Here is life. I have been following death. Here is love. I have become wooden by all my extraordinary exercises. I cannot even do this much good as to relieve the spiritual pain of this good girl. Fie on my philosophy!" And up he rose and lifted the girl up in his lap and began crying with her like an old father. That was manly.

This man seemed to have killed his own good emotions by forcing them down a floor of slabs of philosophic dead finalities of certain curious concepts and mental images about life and death and reality. It was by the touch of her grief that his roots coppiced up, throwing the dead crust of philosophic hardness aside. And he poured out floods. Seeing him weep, all wept. The saint realized his saintship of sympathy and felt a new truth like a new dawn bursting upon a storm of rain and wind.

But philosophy could not help.

A man famed for his religious and psychic knowledge appeared in the famous city, seeking the *Doer of Good* for some funds to spread his new religion all over the earth. He had got a million sovereigns already from the *Doer of Good* and was building his first temple in the city of the *Doer of Good*.

And they took her to this man of new religion. She had those pain-lit eyes, the pain of which moved the trees and birds to tears. But the religious man saw her and preached a sermon and gave her a few books to read and exhorted her to devote her life to the spread of his new religion.

And in his infatuation for the spread of the new religion to relieve humanity, this new apostle realized not that a noble soul had come to the door of a *temple* and found *nothing* there, but books and sermons and, ringing of bells and empty flourishing of lamps and worship of God! And a vain lot of similar fooling!!

Months passed. She was still roaming self-neglected and threadbare, bare-headed, bare-footed, bare-kneed, bare-elbowed crying in the streets, "Why hast thou, O love! not taken me with thee? Why hast thou left me here? How cruel of death that he does not come to me. How cruel of you to have gone away. Thou wouldst not leave me alone even for a single moment. Thou distrusted my body, that it may not slip, it may not fall, it may not drop, it may not be swallowed by day or by night, and here I am still alive. And thou art gone. O God! O God! Where art Thou? Thou art known to be merciful. Unite me with my young prince of beauty."

And when she passed crying, the *Doer of Good* came down from his palace, and began to go bare-footed with her in formal, solemn sympathy, in one more effort to rescue her.

"Why do you come with me, sir?"
"If you could deign to accept my help."
"Yes, please help me to die and to meet my young prince of beauty."
"I can help you to live."
"Yes, please help me to live with him, my young prince of beauty."
"I can offer all my millions and lay them at your feet, but I cannot help you to be united with him. The dead no one can bring back to life, as the day that is past cannot be recalled, as the flame that is blown out cannot be relit!"

"But have your millions the power of bringing back my substance of life—my young prince of beauty?"

"They can provide you with all that life requires, surround you with comforts physical, with new religions, with great old philosophies, with art and artists that create beauty, with songs and songsters who sing to gladden the heart of all creation—all this for you. Deign to accept."

"But I am seeking for death. Of what use to the dead are these things that interest the living?"

"I desire you to work for the good of humanity after I am dead, to continue my work. This is noble enough."

"I am the sufferer. How can I work as the saviour? Leave me alone, sir! Your proposals sicken me. The interval you are creating in my grief will cost me more of personal misery to fill the gaps. Leave me alone, sir."

"How strange is your sorrow that finds no hope in deeds of goodness. Life finds its fulfilment in consecrating itself to do good to others. Some god has constrained us all to this misery; and to help each other put of it is the highest function of ethics, religion, philosophy and humanity. I see no higher object of life."

"God bless you. Go and feed your widows, the miserable wretches who find life worth living for mere clothes and bread provided by you. If they were true women, they would starve to death rather than have godless bread at your hands. Death is better than the life that all your ethics, religions and philanthropies can provide."

"Your very words are cutting my flesh as if with the dull-edged scythes. Please leave me alone."

"She is mad," he thought to himself and went his way.

The princess of sorrow found that her sorrow had dimmed by the talk of the *Doer of Good*. And she sat under a tree and cursed herself for having met him. And her noble grief would not return to her. She felt miserable. And she rose from under the tree still dead, calm and collected, and went away. She did not know where she was. She was dazed, dulled, made much too physical. She felt very heavy as if her knees were made of lead. She went out of the city and saw two birds perching on one branch. A young boy was playing with his *Gulel* and bang flew a stone and killed one. It dropped. And the princess cried, her arms went flying in the air. "O Death! Take not him from me. Stay, stay. Give him back to me." And with this cry the princess regained her sorrow. And she roamed on the paths of life, crying, crying for him.

"Daughter," came the voice from behind her, suddenly, like the thunder of the rain clouds, when the winds blew, the rain fell and the evening came on with hurried, impatient steps, outside the city walls.

"Thy prince of beauty lives!"

"Does he?" said she and fell on the grass, almost faint.

And the simple labourer of the city of the *Doer of Good,* the *Toiler on Earth,* tucked her hair in the centre of her head and breathed over the plaits the name of the Beautiful One. And as he closed his eyes and went on naming the Beautiful One, she slept full of rest. She slept on his knee as did John on the knee of Jesus. As she woke up she said, "I feel comforted."

"Daughter, does the Name resound in the temple of your heart?"

"Yes, sir, it is beautiful. The Name is nectar". And she slept again on his knee. After some minutes she opened her eyes again in wonder.

And enfeebled with the comfort of the soul, she sat on the grass and quivered.

"What numerous black shapes, there!" said she in an indifferent surprise of utter ignorance.

"Where?" said the *Toiler on Earth*.

Towards the right she looked and covered her eyes with her hands.

"They are the forms of misery, the ghosts of darkness come out of you."

"I know. What a terrible self!" She just looked without saying the words.

"What is there? There! There!"

"What seest thou?"

"A tall majestic figure made of light, beautiful long locks, long white beard. I see only the feet. I see only the face. How bright! How soothing! How loving! How consoling! Ah! we are not alone, there are celestial beings, we do not die."

"Yes. You are saved, daughter."

"I feel soothed as if a burning coal had been taken off my heart."

And in the Unseen, the *Toiler on Earth* saw the same cosmic phenomenon which he had seen in dream when he prayed for the comfort of the soul of a widow in Heaven still crying for her husband. And he now saw that he had seen in his former dream this princess separated from her prince of beauty. It was she whom he had comforted by a prayer in his dream, and whose re-union he had seen in Heaven. And he saw vividly how the Master had cancelled all that long and tragic future of her suffering.

As he had touched her tresses a little grain of the substance of life passed out of his bosom into hers and she was healed of sorrow.

Just then a shower of a few big rain-drops fell. The city of the *Doer of Good* had been parched for many days by then. And as he touched the crown of her head, the big drops of cooling rain, two or three large drops fell on her crown and they went dripping through his fingers that were closed over in the form of a lotus-bud blessing her. And she fell into a super-trance.

In her trance the Prophet—appeared to her and showed her the nail marks. "This is how the sick are healed," said the Prophet to her, and he raised his finger towards where yonder stood in shining raiment the *Toiler on Earth,* and the Prophet—said to her pointing to him, "Ye that suffer, rise and suffer less and save him the pain of crucifixion, for he must suffer who saves you."

And seeing this vision she awoke in a new robe of her soul and she felt she was an angel and her prince of youth stood by her side in the spiritual realms and both in the supreme bliss of re-union were gazing with wondrous devotion at that shining face of the *Toiler on Earth.*

Footnotes:

1. This story is based on one of the many such scenes from the life of *Bhai*—, a Sikh apostle, to which I am an eye-witness. Names of all personalities have been suppressed. —*Puran Singh.*

	chapter	Book page, line	Doc page, line
persuation	5 the spiritual	19,27	1,21
,,	6 the garden	51,28	1,47
cony	B Surta	112,9	7,11
persuation	G the brother	154,36	4,28

Made in the USA
Middletown, DE
21 September 2020